IF YOU LIKE
THE SOPRANOS...

IF YOU LIKE

THE SOPRANOS...

HERE ARE **OVER 150** MOVIES, TV SHOWS, AND OTHER ODDITIES THAT YOU WILL LOVE

LEONARD PIERCE

AN IMPRINT OF HAL LEONARD CORPORATION

Published in 2011 by Limelight Editions
An Imprint of Hal Leonard Corporation
7777 West Bluemound Road
Milwaukee, WI 53213

Trade Book Division Editorial Offices
33 Plymouth St., Montclair, NJ 07042

Book design by Michael Kellner

Printed in the United States of America

Library of Congress Cataloging-in-Publication Data
Pierce, Leonard.
   If you like The Sopranos-- : here are over 150 movies, tv shows, and other oddities that you will love / Leonard Pierce.
       p. cm.
   Includes index.
   ISBN 978-0-87910-390-3
   1. Gangster films--United States--History and criticism. 2. Crime films--United States--History and criticism. 3. Gangster television programs--United States--History and criticism. 4. Television crime shows--United States--History and criticism. I. Title.
   PN1995.9.G3P54 2011
   791.43'6556--dc23
                                        2011036580

www.limelighteditions.com

For Cori

CONTENTS

IF YOU LIKE
THE SOPRANOS...

Michael Imperioli and James Gandolfini in *The Sopranos*.
(HBO/Photofest)

Introduction

CRIMINAL MINDED

Crime, that "left-handed form of human endeavor," is one of the most ancient subjects in every form of art. When the first human defined something as his property, the second figured out a way to steal it from him—and the third told a sensationalized version of the theft to the fourth. Our myths, our histories, even our religions are filled with stories of brutal murders, audacious robberies, and daring schemes. The Bible contains innumerable stories of crime: beginning with Cain, the first murderer, this holy text that defines itself by a set of ten inflexible laws constantly concerns itself with the people who set out to break them. The myths and religions of other cultures, from the Far East to the heart of Africa, are no less populated with folk heroes, tricksters, and villains who are expert at various forms of criminal enterprise. From Robin Hood and his Merry Men to the Chinese bandit leader Pei Yuanshao to the bloody aftermath of *Macbeth*, fictional lawbreakers have been both celebrated and vilified in every era.

And as long as there have been criminals, both real and imagined, there have been people to tell stories about them. Writers, poets, musicians, artists, and playwrights have been consistently fascinated by the dark underbelly of civilization since the first city walls went up. Endless lines have been written about real-world murderers, thieves, and gangs, from the original Thugs of India to the shocking murders of Jack the Ripper; when the storytellers lacked actual criminals to mythologize, they simply made them up. Criminals, who prey on our worst fears about human nature while remaining indistinguishable from us, stand in stark contrast to enemies in war, or abstractions like monsters or demons. Criminals win our sympathy and understanding because it is all too easy to see how we could have taken that selfsame path; but they also inspire terror and dread because they refuse to play by the civilized rules we've come up with to convince ourselves that we are on an ever-improving path to progress. Artists understand this contradiction more than most, and that is why they have been obsessed with crime since the dawn of history. The brilliant science-fiction author Samuel R. Delany put it this way: "The only important elements in any society are the artistic and the criminal, because they alone, by questioning the society's values, can force it to change."

In 1999, a serial drama appeared on the HBO network that would utterly transform not only the ages-old tradition of the crime drama, but also the medium of television. *The Sopranos*, created by TV veteran David Chase, came at exactly the right time. It appeared in the waning days of the twentieth century, only a few years before a criminal act that would define the new millennium: a savage terrorist attack on New York. The attack shocked Americans into a new cultural era, in which *The Sopranos* was simultaneously the culmination of hundreds of cultural trends and artifacts that had come before and an entirely new addition to the artistic landscape. The purpose of this book is to provide an incomplete but hopefully illuminating portrait of those elements that came together to create the stellar artistic achievement that is *The Sopranos*—and to follow the new trails it left in the sky when it exploded into the cultural consciousness, heralding the arrival of a new era of storytelling.

It is only appropriate that David Chase's magnificent creation appeared when it did, in the dying days of the twentieth century. The 1900s had been an incredibly fruitful time for the art form for which we use the cultural shorthand of "crime drama." To begin with, it was the media age: photography came into its own, the development of recording technology allowed music to be spread all over the world, motion pictures turned out to be a medium tailor-made for crime stories, and broadcast media—radio and television—would create millions of new consumers of entertainment, who would respond just as favorably to tales of murder and mayhem as their ancestors had. The growth of lightning-fast communication via the telegram, telephone, and Internet meant that news stories could be disseminated all over the planet in a matter of seconds; and the news, following the "If it bleeds, it leads" dictum of sensationalistic journalism, was always full of stories about crime. Stories (both actual and invented) that previously would have been known only to locals became worldwide sensations, and listeners and viewers hungry for entertainment formed an eager audience for those stories—the bloodier, the better.

But it wasn't merely developments in media and technology that made the 1900s the Century of Crime. New media provided the means, but reality was all too eager to supply the material. The twentieth century saw several key developments that led to the proliferation of what would come to be termed "organized crime." The nearly universal spread of consumer capitalism provided the motive, since its inherent qualities of inequity ensured there would always be those on the outside looking to get in, and willing to cut corners to do it. Urbanization—the shift of global populations from rural areas to big cities—gave criminals not only a plethora of victims to exploit and terrorize, but also a customer base of those looking for goods and services they couldn't get legitimately, or at the right price. Shifting patterns of immigration helped create a global economy, and areas once thought of as culturally homogenous became multicultural and diverse; ethnic groups brought with them old traditions of secrecy and insularity, and their difficulty in breaking into traditional avenues of success made them all too willing to engage in criminal enterprises. Overproduction of consumer goods, easy access to weapons, corruption in the ranks of politicians and law enforcement, and an increased demand for illicit substances all played their part, and before too long, organized crime was present in almost every big city in the world. Never before in history had crime been so widespread, so coordinated, or so powerful. At times, it seemed as if organized crime was more effective—and more reliable—than local governments.

Organized lawlessness took on many forms in the Century of Crime. Old West outlaw gangs, narco-terrorists, tongs, triads, street thugs, high-seas pirates, human traffickers, smugglers, cybercriminals, bootleggers, counterfeiters, and crews of bank robbers and contract killers all plagued the population. Many of these were organized along ethnic lines, dumping Old World hatreds and regional factionalism into America's melting pot; but just as many were unaffiliated groups of hoodlums whose only common quality was a desire to make a lot of money and no qualms about how to do it.

Of all the organized criminal groups that have seized the public imagination, though, none have proven so durable—both as a going concern in the real world and a compelling myth in the public imagination—as the Italian outfit variously referred to as the Mafia, *La Cosa Nostra*, or simply "the mob." Growing out of various small-time gangs of extortionists and petty criminals in the Old World, this organization first appeared during a great wave of Italian immigration to America and England during the latter part of the nineteenth and early part of the twentieth century. Originally composed of petty blackmailers and strong-arm artists collectively known as the Black Hand, it grew into a force to be reckoned with as more Italian immigration created new opportunities for illegal income, but not until Prohibition did it become a national power in the United States. The vast amount of money to be made in the bootleg liquor trade in the 1920s led the Italian criminals to shed their small-time rivalries and organize into perhaps the most powerful crime syndicate ever seen, and it was during this period that the Mafia developed its reputation as capable of both massive moneymaking prowess and unspeakable violence.

Why the Mafia, of all organized crime outfits, so attracted the fancy of the American public can be attributed to a number of factors. Of course, during the "golden era" of the American mob, when Al Capone and his cronies were making headlines every day, they were impossible to ignore: they made so much money, took so many lives, and so thoroughly suborned the criminal justice system that they demanded international attention. This is not to say there weren't people who tried to ignore them: J. Edgar Hoover, longtime head of the Federal Bureau of Investigation, famously downplayed any investigation into organized crime, even going as far as to deny there was any such thing as the Mafia. The reason for his reluctance is still hotly debated, but the fact remains that, until events overtook him and made the existence of *La Cosa Nostra* impossible to ignore, Hoover chose to focus the attention of the country's most powerful law enforcement agency on individual bank robbers, subversive political groups, and people who challenged his grasp on power. The FBI would eventually prove to be the Mafia's greatest foe, but this didn't happen on Hoover's watch; his denial of what everyone else couldn't help but notice only added to the legend and prestige of the mob.

But other factors were also at play in the Mafia's long monopoly on the nation's cultural imagination. Italians were one of the largest groups of immigrants to the United States, especially in big, media-saturated East Coast cities; everyone knew an Italian-American, and the possibility that that person might be involved in some nefarious activity was both repulsive and perversely appealing. Unlike the socially undesirable African-American gangs or the entirely alien Chinese tongs and triads, Mafiosi arose from a European background that was comprehensible and at least slightly respectable, but their secretive rituals and hostility toward outsiders gave them just enough of an exotic quality to make them fascinating. Their origins in a country at the very heart of Catholicism provided an intriguing contradiction, as men who professed to be devoutly religious engaged in rampant thievery, brutality, and murder. The Mafia, perhaps more than any other criminal organization, proved flexible, adapting to changing times (its members were able to avoid disaster when Prohibition's repeal cut off their primary source of income) and channeling huge amounts of ill-gotten gain into legitimate businesses. Their ability to insinuate themselves into mainstream society was unprecedented for a criminal syndicate; they exercised a perilous degree of control over the union movement for decades, and are widely believed to have played a key role in the election of at least one president (and, for that matter, the death of that same president). Their great and ostentatious wealth, combined with their taste for highly public and bloody violence, as well as all the aforementioned factors, placed them first and foremost in the public imagination whenever organized crime was discussed.

Other cultural factors played into the public fascination with the Mafia. The ancient tribal hatreds and arcane rituals that formed part of mob lore arose from a nation that had brought us not only the savage conquests of Rome and the internecine scheming of the Borgias, but also the Renaissance and the Florentine Camerata. The turbulent history of twentieth-century Italian politics had introduced the abuses of Mussolini's Fascist government, but had also brought a wave of incredibly hardworking and patriotic immigrants to America. And the Catholic traditions that pumped through Italy from the heart of Rome, too, reflected both terrible bloodshed and ineffable beauty. Italian artists, from the peerless elegance of the Florentine School to the observant Realist filmmakers of the '40s and '50s, had always found a way to present a balance between the divine glory with which mankind was suffused and the crude earthiness that kept it separate from its heavenly origins. It would not be long before a generation of filmmakers—Catholic, Italian-American, educated but of working-class origin, and artistic but fascinated with the more prosaic side of their surroundings—would emerge and define the Mafia epic as a central part of American culture.

These men—among them Francis Ford Coppola, Martin Scorsese, and David Chase (born David DeCesare in a New York town just across the border from the Bronx)—were perceptive and intelligent artists, who were nonetheless obsessed with the allure of criminal violence that consumed so many of their peers and relatives; they were of it, but not in it. In the deadly pettiness of turf wars and mob clashes, they saw an echo of the Caesars, a desire to reify the glory that was Rome on a self-mockingly small scale. Their perceptions would be filtered through Hollywood, but were distinctly New York: nowhere else had the mob set itself up so thoroughly into the thread of everyday life, and nowhere else did the

Mafia have the power and will to divide a whole city amongst five "families," like medieval princes carving up a conquered fiefdom. (California is present in their myth, but is often portrayed as a place where the normal rules of reality do not apply, an exotic El Dorado.) Their intelligence, artistic tendencies, and keen observational skills allowed them to see the contradictions and ironies that eluded the people they watched: the way mobsters grew rich exploiting the people they claimed to be defending ("protection," they called it); the overarching importance of family to men who cheated on their wives and tore other families apart through violence and predation; the grand conflict of the sacred and the profane, where gangsters would mouth pieties and donate ostentatiously to the Church, while making their living off of mortal sins.

It was these men who most completely installed the Mafia and its tropes into our collective cultural understanding. And it was David Chase who distilled the two purest extracts of this cultural concoction—its unhinged violence, painted in garish primary colors, and its gray, shaded psychology, hidden in the shadows and never discussed—into a single program: *The Sopranos*. If you are reading this book, it's because, like millions of people all over the world, *The Sopranos* struck home with you, as that rarest of popular entertainment that provides genuine insight into the way ordinary people live their lives while transforming the very medium in which it is presented. *The Sopranos* is unmistakably a work of singular genius, but every work of singular genius has precedents, and every work of singular genius leaves echoes that are heard by others and interpreted in new and equally singular ways. This book's goal is to walk you through some of the films and television shows that provided the building blocks of what became *The Sopranos*, and to point you toward some of the more interesting entertainment churned up in its wake. If you like *The Sopranos*, this book will discuss where it came from and where it led, and hopefully, you will find much to like in those directions as well.

As discussed, the twentieth century was the Century of Crime—but it was also the Century of Film. Moviemaking is the definitive art form of the 1900s, the first unique artistic medium to appear during the period and the one that made the greatest mark during its run. We will begin, then, with the early days of motion pictures, with early examples of the big-screen crime drama, with the coming of the Hays Code and how it changed the moral tenor of movie bad guys, and some early examples of the guilt, dread, and longing that would show up in *The Sopranos* around seventy years later. We'll move on to the rise of film noir, with its psychological depth, its dark sense of despair, and the way it was used by filmmakers to push back against the restrictions of the code with cleverly concealed violence and sexuality. We'll move through the turbulent period of the 1950s and 1960s, looking at the rise of heist films and caper movies, the growing presence of crime drama in international cinema, and the way the fluctuating moral standards of the era gave rise to a new generation of filmmakers. And we'll examine the social and cultural factors that led up to the making of *The Godfather*, the definitive mob epic and the foundational document of *The Sopranos*.

We'll go on to discuss the mob movie in decline, profound shifts in the tone and makeup of crime dramas, the self-reflexive nostalgia that crept into stories of organized crime, and the ins and outs of *GoodFellas*, which is to *The Sopranos* as the New Testament is to the Bible. Developments in multiculturalism, postmodernism, comic reversal, and social upheaval will be examined, until we arrive at *The Sopranos'* year zero, as well as other important factors at work in the portrayal of crime on the big and small screen starting in 1999. From there, we'll focus on television—not just how *The Sopranos* transformed serial storytelling in home entertainment, but the shows that came before it, the ones that followed it, and the way *its* techniques and approach spilled over into other media, especially the world of video games. Along the way, we'll help you track the careers of the people who made them so meaningful and compelling.

Rarely in the history of a single artistic medium does a show as game-changing as *The Sopranos* come around. It received so much praise in its initial run that it was almost off-putting; but now that it has ended, no amount of critical hype seems excessive, and it is impossible to watch television without seeing endless echoes of David Chase's storytelling approach. Hopefully, *If You Like The Sopranos*... will not only enhance your enjoyment of a magnificent work of art that you already know and love, but also open up new paths leading into and away from it that will prove equally rewarding and equally full of potential. Tony Soprano wasn't just the head of a biological family and a boss of a crime family—he was a member of one of the richest and most fascinating cultural families of the modern era. Now it's time to meet the rest of that family.

James Cagney in *White Heat*. (Warner Bros. Pictures Inc./Photofest)

1

BIG IDEAS:
EARLY HOLLYWOOD GANGSTERS

WHITE HEAT

If you divide the Century of Crime the same way almost everything else in the twentieth century is divided—into a convenient dichotomy of pre— and post–World War II— then you can get a fairly clear view of how crime dramas developed in Hollywood and elsewhere: first came the silent film era, with its melodramatic gangsters; then the explosion of urban crime dramas during the 1920s, mirroring the growth of organized crime during Prohibition; the gangster epics of the '30s and the moral panic that led to the adoption of the Hays Code; and the pushback that gave rise to the noir period during and immediately after the war. Then, the dividing line; and in the '50s came caper and heist films, followed by more socially relevant and psychologically complex crime movies in the '60s, the mob epics of the '70s, grittier and gorier fare in the '80s, and the great decline that culminated, just as the century came to a close, in *The Sopranos*.

Like all simple cultural shorthand, though, this scheme has its flaws. This becomes obvious when viewing the classic-era gangster movie that probably influenced the story of Tony Soprano more than any other: 1949's *White Heat*. For one thing, it feels like a classic gangster film of the '30s, somehow transplanted forward in time to the period where noir held sway. Second, it stars James Cagney —who, while indisputably a gangster icon, was in the autumn of his career, having delivered many of his unforgettable bad-guy roles more than a decade before. The movie's characters are partly based on Ma Barker's gang, a filial group of hoods who committed their crimes in the early 1930s; and the train job that kicks off the film is patterned after a robbery that took place in 1923. Finally, it was directed—with great skill and an unexpected degree of depth, but in a decidedly retro style—by Raoul Walsh, who made his first gangster film all the way back in 1915. All of this points to *White Heat* as a throwback, a retrogression to a vanished period of gangster movies—not something that stood at the precipice of the noir era and dared to look decades ahead.

But it's one of those contradictions that makes for perfection. The old-fashioned qualities of *White Heat* might have masked or even buried its complexity and force, but instead, they enhanced those qualities, and threw the film into sharp relief against the shadows. Walsh—a masterful director of crime dramas who will appear many more times in this book—attached the psychologically rich characters of the noir era to his technically solid old-school approach; and Cagney, having learned a trick or two in the '30s, absolutely burns up the screen as unhinged mobster Cody Jarrett. The result is a film that seems like it is from one era while acrobatically spanning two—and one that establishes some powerful themes that would later be reincarnated in the world of Tony Soprano.

Jarrett is the leader of a heist gang, and Cagney—fifty years old at the time—plays him with the manic energy of a man half his age. After pulling off a train robbery in which they brutally murder four men, Jarrett's gang holes up in the woods, waiting for a chance to escape a police dragnet. Tensions run remarkably high, not only because of their fear of being caught, but also because Jarrett is clearly going insane. His violent behavior would be bad enough (he leaves a wounded comrade to freeze to death, and beats another for listening to the radio), but he's also prone to screaming fits as the result of devastating headaches. No one in the gang thinks he's a particularly good leader, but they also live in mortal fear of him; only "Big Ed" Somers (Steve Cochran) plots to take over one day. Jarrett is well aware of this, and sneeringly mocks Somers and his "big ideas," The only person Jarrett truly relates to is his mother, played by veteran British actress Margaret Wycherly. A shrewd and calculating woman, she helps steer her son's career while undercutting his gang and belittling his wife, Verna (Virginia Mayo). Jarrett dotes on his mother, and he brutalizes his wife when Verna dares to criticize her. ☞

SUPPORTING EVIDENCE: 5 MORE FASCINATING FILMS FROM THE CLASSIC CRIME ERA

1. ***The Penalty*** (1920, USA; Wallace Worsley, dir.)

Drawn from the pulp tradition, this silent film—starring horror movie legend Lon Chaney Sr.—isn't just atypical for a gangster film, it's downright bizarre. Chaney plays Blizzard, a criminal mastermind (and accidental amputee) who runs San Francisco's underworld and enslaves women to make bootleg hats!

2. ***I Am a Fugitive from a Chain Gang*** (1932, USA; Mervyn LeRoy, dir.)

A wave of prison movies were released following the success of 1930's *The Big House*, but none were more memorable than this stark tale of Southern law. Paul Muni is tremendous as a war veteran who can never escape the repercussions of an unjust conviction for robbery; the final scene is unforgettable.

3. ***Wild Boys of the Road*** (1933, USA; William Wellman, dir.)

An instructive look at the kind of films made during the Depression, before the brutal edge entered the gangster film, this film is focused on the hard-luck adventures of a group of impoverished kids riding the rails. Its sentimental ending is typical of the soft touch once common in crime dramas.

4. ***Angels with Dirty Faces*** (1938, USA; Michael Curtiz, dir.)

The Hays Code had a huge impact on the overall tone of gangster films, as evidenced by the famous ending of this successful morality play. James Cagney and Pat O'Brien play childhood friends who get mixed up in crime, but O'Brien reforms and becomes a priest, while Cagney remains an unrepentant criminal.

5. ***Dillinger*** (1945, USA; Max Nosseck, dir.)

One of the last classic gangster movies before the rise of film noir,

Dillinger tells the story of one of the period's most notorious criminals, played by legendary Hollywood hard man Lawrence Tierney. The screenplay, by crackerjack writer Philip Yordan (*The Big Combo*), was nominated for an Oscar.

So enormous is the latest crime pulled by the Jarrett mob, leaving so many dead and pulling in $300,000 in cash (a gargantuan take in 1949), that no one can avoid the dragnet for long. Hoping to meet up with a fence in Los Angeles, Jarrett learns that the heat is on, and scrambles to figure out what to do next. As his mother calculates and conspires, urging him to cut out everyone she deems dangerous (that is, everyone), he takes as few chances as possible. After nearly being caught by a patrol car outside of an L.A. drive-in—Jarrett even drives like a lunatic—he decides to turn himself in for a crime he didn't commit, which will not only net him a shorter sentence, but also provide him with an airtight alibi for the train robbery, leaving his cohorts to dangle.

The cops aren't quite as stupid as Jarrett thinks, though, and before long, the T-men have placed one of their own in his cell—undercover specialist Hank Fallon (Edmond O'Brien), whose job is to befriend Jarrett and milk him for information about how he managed to launder all the train robbery loot. On the outside, Big Ed puts some of his big ideas into action, arranging for a fellow con to take out Jarrett—a plan sabotaged when Fallon saves Cody's life, creating a tight bond between the two. Ma Jarrett tips her son to Big Ed's treachery, but she pays the price: Verna, who's gone over to Ed's side, puts a bullet in her back. News of her death sends Jarrett into a psychotic rage in one of the film's many iconic scenes; he takes hostages, busts out of prison (with Fallon in tow), and delivers a brutal revenge on the man who tried to kill him, as well as Big Ed.

Reassembling his gang, Jarrett plans another big job: a payroll robbery at a gas works in Long Beach. Things go wrong when Fallon, exposed by a new member of the gang, reveals his status as a snitch. The police surround the place, and everyone either surrenders or is killed. Jarrett, robbed of his mother and betrayed by everyone who ever pretended to care for him, suffers a complete break with reality. Atop a treacherously flammable gas container and surrounded by police snipers, he goes berserk, screaming the toast he once shared with his mother in good times ("Top of the world!") before his final immolation in a gout of flame. This unforgettable ending helped seal the movie's reputation as an instant classic.

White Heat had fifty years to settle in as an iconic gangster film before *The Sopranos* appeared, but it is still shocking how close the parallels are between the two. David Chase doesn't do anything as crass as steal directly from the story of Cody Jarrett, but he borrows enough elements from it to make *The Sopranos* a fun-house mirror version. While Tony is more passive and thoughtful than Cody, he's equally distrustful and contemptuous of his underlings, and just as brutal when he feels that his fatherly affections have been spurned. He may treat Carmela better than Cody treats Verna, but he doesn't value her much more, and never sticks up for her when his mother heaps calumnies upon her. Cody's shrieking fits and stabbing headaches are mirrored by Tony's anxiety attacks, and they're both quick to suspect betrayal even when none has taken place. (As Verna hisses when the cops first track Jarrett down, "It's always 'Somebody tipped them,' never 'The cops are smart.'") Cody Jarrett, the thug twisted by psychotic episodes and warped by a misguided mutation of motherly love, lies somewhere between the traditional greed-driven tough guy of old-school gangster movies and the maniacal murderers of the post-*Psycho* era, and Tony Soprano perfectly manifests that branch of character. *White Heat* also manages to highlight, within the confines of what was allowed by the Hays Code, the difficult relationship between cops and criminals, and the brutal emotional toll paid by both the men who pretend friendship to get their prey and the crooks who learn that they can trust no one, no matter how close the bond.

But it is Cody Jarrett's relationship with his mother that forms the most obvious parallel between *White Heat* and *The Sopranos*.

There are clear similarities in the twisted Oedipal bond between the two, and there are divergences that are just as clear; at times, the relationship between Cody and Ma Jarrett reads like a bizarre what-could-have-been take on the relationship between Tony and Livia Soprano. Both women are resentful, even contemptuous, of their son's wives, although Verna takes a far more aggressive approach toward handling her mother-in-law than does Carmela. Both mothers are revealed to have played a role in their husbands' downfall—Tony's father, Johnny-Boy, was henpecked and undermined at every turn by Livia, while Ma Jarrett played a part in Cody's father's criminal career, which ended with his ignominious death in an insane asylum. But where Tony's mother continued taking out her dissatisfaction with her own life on her son after her husband was gone, Cody's mother ruined her child the opposite way: pushing him to succeed in the brutal life that destroyed her husband. Livia gives Tony no support, questioning his every decision and drowning out his personality in the tide of her own misery. Ma Jarrett, on the other hand, is *too* supportive of her son, destroying all the relationships he has with anyone but her, and encouraging him to distrust his gang, leading him to think that only she can be trusted and believed. It's fascinating to watch the show and the movie in close proximity, and to speculate what Tony might have become had his life been dominated by a Ma Jarrett rather than a Livia Soprano. It would have been different, but it might not have been any happier.

It is a fascinating parallel, and one that leaves plenty of credit to go around to the writers who created the women, the directors who filled them out, and the actresses who brought them to life. The mother figures in most movies of the classic Hollywood era—even those in crime films—are sentimental creations, matronly weepers with hearts of gold, melted into sickly pools by the tragic bad behavior of their darling boys. But Ma Jarrett is a new creation, a Machiavellian schemer who claims to love her son, but steers him toward cruelty and vice, and who encourages him to trust no one but her.

There are, of course, more parallels between the two: *White*

Heat's clever structure places a lot of value on the form that would become known as the police procedural, letting us behind the scenes to see how law enforcement agents make a case against criminals. *The Sopranos* was never a police procedural (though it is close to being a crime procedural), but it drew deeply from the well of that genre in some of its best episodes. For a movie made during the studio era, *White Heat* also places a lot of importance on location and geographical verisimilitude (its Los Angeles locations are expertly selected, and an early chase scene takes us through a number of areas that are still around today). David Chase, too, strived to accurately portray not only the mobsters of New Jersey, but also the place as a character. Watching it today, it is difficult to say who deserves more credit: David Chase, for looking so far back for inspiration for a television show that defined its era; or Raoul Walsh, for looking so far ahead in crafting a movie that seemed to be both a throwback to a previous era of filmmaking and a preview of what was to come.

REGENERATION AND THE SILENT ERA

Hollywood was literally born into crime. This was not only true in the sense that some of the earliest silent films dealt with lawless go-ings-on, from urban gangster tales to stories of Wild West outlaws (some of whom were still alive when the movies came out), but also in that the early moviemakers were often quite literally criminals themselves. Unwilling to pay the hefty license fees demanded by Thomas Edison, who held patents on the process of filmmaking, many directors moved westward to avoid the agents he sent to seize their equipment. Los Angeles was a wild place at the time, little more than a Wild West town itself; filmmakers would hide their cameras in safes or under beds, or film at night to avoid the prying eyes of the Pinkerton detectives in Edison's employ.

One reason the western proved so popular as a genre in the early days of Hollywood was that America, still largely ruralized, could relate to stories of bandits, outlaws, and desperados more than it could to urban gangsters. Even then, movies and moral panic walked hand in hand: 1903's *The Great Train Robbery* (released at a time when real train robberies were not uncommon) featured a scene judged too unnerving for audiences, in which a bandit points his gun at the camera. But change was in the air, and the passage of alcohol prohibition in 1920—and the subsequent rise of gangster-ism to fill the void left by legitimate channels of alcohol distribu-tion—meant that the gangster movie was well on its way. It would become one of the essential archetypes of American entertain-ment. By the 1920s, gangster films like *Underworld* and *Thunderbolt* were making small fortunes; even the first all-talking picture, *Lights of New York*, was a crime drama.

But it would be wrong to divide the movies of the '10s and '20s into so simple a western/gangster divide. Pioneering filmmaker D. W. Griffith made a proto-gangster movie in 1912 with the absurdly pleasing title *The Musketeers of Pig Alley*, as did Cecil B. DeMille a few years later with *Kindling*. One of the most significant of the crime films of the period was 1915's *Regeneration*. It was directed by Raoul Walsh, whose career behind the camera lasted fifty years and produced many outstanding crime films. Besides *White Heat*, Walsh was responsible for the gangster film *The Roaring Twenties* (discussed later in this book) and the films noir *They Drive by Night* and *High Sierra*. *Regeneration*, the story of an orphaned boy who rises to lead a gang before being reformed by the love of a good woman, was quite well made, but it was in many ways typical of the drama, criminal and otherwise, of its peculiar era. Seeking mass appeal (and wanting to avoid the attention of the censors), it minimized the wrongdoing and violence and pumped up the melodrama. But, in conjunction with other urban crime films, it helped pave the way for the breathtaking, bloody gangster classics of the 1930s, and as such, is an important precedent for *The Sopranos*.

SCARFACE AND THE PRE-CODE CLASSICS

Moviegoers of the 1930s were, often as not, trapped in a miasma of despair: the Great Depression was in full swing, jobs were scarce, and poverty was on the increase, while bootleggers and mob boss-es growing fat off of Prohibition resorted to more and bloodier violence to protect their ill-gotten gains. And yet audiences never shrank from the portrayal of these realities on screen; even film fans who lived in areas dominated by brutal gangsters flocked to movie theaters to see fictionalized versions of the criminals work their evil magic.

Before the adaptation of the Motion Picture Production Code—whose imprint became necessary in 1934 to release a movie in the United States, and which was popularly named for Will Hays, its chief enforcer—America had fallen in love with its gangster films. Pre-Code films seem largely tame by today's standards, but their depiction of scantily clad women, drug use, and—particularly in the case of gangster films—over-the-top violence set off a moral panic. Church groups (especially the Catholic Legion of Decency) united with social activists, many of whom had also backed Prohibition, to demand the adoption of a censorship code to prevent what they perceived as the widespread corruption of juveniles by the movies.

The pre-Code era had seen an ever-increasing rise in the popularity of gangster movies, and there's no question that the tough-guy attitudes of many of the nation's urban youth were influenced by the big-screen characters they emulated, though it's doubtful their rebellion went much further than making lippy comments to their parents, much less took them all the way into a life of crime. Three movies in particular are cited as especially egregious (or admirable) and have become known as the classics of the pre-Code crime drama era. 1931's *Little Caesar* told a resonant gangster story and made a huge star out of Edward G. Robinson. *The Public Enemy* did the same that year for the sneering, abusive James Cagney—and made a fool out of Will Hays, who predicted its failure, based on the notion that audiences were tiring of gangster films. But the movie that may have done more than any other to spur the adoption of the Code was 1932's *Scarface*.

Incredibly influential, and frequently remade, this barely veiled telling of the rise of Al Capone was always meant to provoke. Director Howard Hawks knew he'd have to go up against Hays, and decided to make *Scarface* as gory as possible; he paid his crew to think up creative and violent murders for each of the victims in the script, and coaxed monstrous performances out of his leads, Paul Muni and George Raft. As the icing on his blood-red cake, he played up the creepy, almost incestuous love between Muni's character and his sister. The predicted censorship conflicts immediately came to pass; after years of battles, two versions of *Scarface*—neither representing Hawks' wishes for the final cut—were released, and instantly drew the expected accusations of glorifying gangsters. It was a fierce battle, and one that would continue to be fought for decades.

EDWARD G. ROBINSON, ORIGINAL GANGSTER

Though Tony Soprano may have worshiped at the altar of Jimmy Cagney, his real prototype was more likely a squat, unpleasant-looking man with a distinctive voice, named Emanuel Goldenberg. In contrast to Cagney's all-American image, the man who would rename himself Edward G. Robinson was a Romanian-born Jew raised in a Yiddish-speaking neighborhood until he was ten years old. And contrary to Cagney's pugnacious off-screen identity as a scrappy individualist forever battling his studio, Robinson was a well-liked, quiet intellectual and art collector who made many friends during his long studio career. But both actors were both small, strong-willed men who carved out a niche for themselves playing tough guys and hoodlums, and both worked in both pre- and post-Code Hollywood and weathered many changes in the film industry to craft long and successful careers.

Robinson had appeared in nearly a dozen features by 1931, but that was the year he became a real star with his unforgettable turn as Caesar Enrico Bandello in *Little Caesar*—the "Rico" who allegedly lent his name to the RICO (Racketeer Influenced and Corrupt Organizations) anti–organized crime act that so plagues Tony Soprano and his associates. Upstart crime boss Rico's vicious, violent cockiness and unforgettable on-screen demise makes him one of the most memorable portrayals of a gangster in the early days of Hollywood, and it's a testament to Robinson's skill as an actor that he wasn't forever stereotyped as a mobster from then on.

Still, even when he played a good guy, Robinson maintained elements of the bad guy in his acting. Playing the role of a chump in Fritz Lang's 1945 film noir *Scarlet Street*, he shows elements of desperation, the air of a man who might do something unspeakably violent if pushed a little too far; and in his outstanding turn as a canny insurance investigator in *Double Indemnity*, the quintessential noir from the previous year, his brilliance, cockiness, and calculated cynicism about human nature would be perfectly suited to any one of the characters he'd played who lived on the other side of the law. Like Tony Soprano, Robinson often appeared as a man who overcame his physical appearance, winning over women with his power and aura of dreadful authority. And, like Tony, his characters were full of bluster and confidence that often masked internal depths of dread and fear. Robinson was well aware of what made him such a formidable on-screen presence. "Some people have youth, some have beauty," he is famously quoted as observing. "I have menace."

His greatest role might just be that of Johnny Rocco, the unspeakably cruel mobster he played in 1949's *Key Largo*. In it, he is an exiled crime boss, attempting a comeback after years of living in Cuba. Overflowing with contempt for the little men who forced him out, longing for his vanished days of power, and sublimating his fear and uncertainty into savage manipulation of his henchmen and his mistress, Robinson's Rocco a terrifying portrait of a criminal—and one that should be familiar to fans of *The Sopranos*.

BRIGHTON ROCK AND CATHOLIC GUILT

Justly or not, the perception of organized crime as a field dominated by Italian-Americans—and, therefore, Catholics—has dominated the stories our culture has told about it. The ties between the Mafia and the Catholic Church have featured in the real world as well, reaching their crescendo in the 1982 Banco Ambrosiano scandal, and mob epics since *The Godfather* have played with the paradox of violent behavior on the part of professedly religious men against a backdrop of Catholic iconography. This template suffuses *The Sopranos*: Tony retains some sense of his church-taught morality, believing that hell is reserved for other people, even though he's a thief and a killer. His daughter Meadow's rebellious godlessness frustrates her parents, and son's A.J.'s status as a mob scion protects him from the consequences of his bad behavior at his Catholic school. Carmela struggles to balance her fear of falling from grace with God against the material comforts achieved by her husband's life of crime, and shows a profound lack of curiosity about Tony's wicked deeds, but is downright appalled when her friends consider divorce. Even the local priest, Father Phil, is shown as a well-meaning but morally compromised figure.

Long before there was a Tony Soprano, though, there was a Pinkie Brown. Pinkie is the teenage hoodlum who stands furiously at the center of British novelist Graham Greene's electrifying crime story *Brighton Rock*, and like so many of Greene's characters, he is a figure standing in the long shadow of the Catholic Church. Greene could not do anything as easy as make a Catholic hero and a godless villain. In *Brighton Rock*, the hero is the good-time girl Ida, who worships only the rough physicality of being alive; the victim is Rose, a Catholic whose devoutness borders on the simpleminded; and the villain is Pinkie, who believes in Catholicism only insofar as its negative qualities are concerned. When Rose proves to be a key witness to a murder for which Pinkie is responsible, he weds her— but he loathes her, despises the sham of a marriage, and doesn't believe in heaven or salvation. His deepest faith is in hell, in pain and eternal punishment. Unlike Tony, he knows he's going to hell, and almost seems to look forward to it, as long as he can send plenty of other people there ahead of him.

Brighton Rock has twice been made into a movie: once in 1947, as a British adaptation with a young Richard Attenborough putting in a sharp-edged performance as Pinkie, and again in 2011, with Ida effectively portrayed by Helen Mirren. The former is the better of the two, with a savvy noir sensibility, but they both soft-pedal the book's horrifying ending, and the more recent version treats the vital Catholic struggle at the heart of the novel far too lightly, as well as requiring some plot acrobatics by moving the setting from the '30s to the '60s. The novel remains the best telling of the story, and sheds light on the conflict between faith and crime that saturates the world of Tony Soprano.

THE ROARING TWENTIES
AND THE END OF THE CLASSICAL ERA

Cultural chauvinism leads many modern audiences to think that homage, parody, and ironic tribute as a relatively recent development in film. *The Roaring Twenties*, a 1939 gangster classic from Warner Brothers, proves otherwise. It's a true classic—smart, well acted, cleverly constructed, and funny—and though posterity hasn't placed it in the first tier of '30s crime dramas, it is extremely worthwhile for a number of reasons.

The story is a pretty straightforward one: three World War I buddies—luckless nice guy Eddie (James Cagney), egotistical tough guy George (Humphrey Bogart), and straight arrow Lloyd (Jeffrey Lynn)—find themselves embroiled in the bootleg hooch trade during Prohibition, all approaching it from different angles. After a series of love triangles and double crosses, the bad guys receive their comeuppance—Bogart with a sense of righteousness and Cagney with a tinge of tragedy. But it's not so much the plot that makes *The Roaring Twenties* such a keystone in the history of crime films; it's the historical moment in which it appeared, and its alert sense of self-awareness.

Directed by Raoul Walsh—who had been behind the camera for *Regeneration*, arguably the first real gangster picture, and who would go on to helm *White Heat*, one of the last echoes of the traditional crime drama—*The Roaring Twenties* appeared at a time when the genre was in a serious state of flux. The influence of the Hays Code had put the kibosh on some of the excess of the old-school gangster epic, and the repeal of Prohibition in 1933 was changing the way organized criminals went about their deadly business. An increasingly cynical public, having been shocked into the harsh realities of the twentieth century by the mass slaughters of World War I, was beginning to suspect they'd have to do it all over again, as war loomed once more in Europe. One of the most fascinating things about *The Roaring Twenties* is that it recognized all these realities and built wry commentary about them around a very traditional gangland narrative.

The Roaring Twenties goes about its work with a maximum of irony: Cagney is such a nice guy, he orders milk in a speakeasy. A florid opening voice-over in the classical style waxes nostalgic about a bygone era—which had ended less than a decade before the movie was made. Everyone's fate conforms to the new demands of the Code, while in the background, scantily clad flappers do their thing. Bootleggers serve up filthy home brew from their bathtubs, and fool all of their customers with a fancy new label. It's all very exciting in the grand old style, while allowing clever viewers plenty of chances to see where it's giving them a knowing wink. By the time *The Roaring Twenties* is over, it is understood as not just a classic—and a tribute to the classics that have gone before—but also a passing of the torch from the Cagney-style gangster to the Bogart-style antihero, and a vital moment in the shift from the '30s gangster movie to the '40s film noir.

Richard Conte and Jean Wallace in *The Big Combo*.
(Allied Artists Pictures Corporation/Photofest)

2

FIRST IS FIRST AND SECOND IS NOBODY: THE RISE OF FILM NOIR

THE BIG COMBO

The next major development in crime movies, after the sentimental stories of the silent era and the explosive, controversial gangster films of the pre-Code era, was the rise of film noir. The evocative name, conjuring up both the black pools of shadow in which the films took place and the black pits of despair that were the doomed protagonists' souls, was actually applied by French film critics years after the movies were made. (Most Americans used the phrase "crime drama," which this book also favors for its generality and wide utility.) But it fit like a well-tailored suit, and noir's unforgettable style and subversive approach made it a favorite genre of critics and filmmakers alike, with new interpretations and applications still appearing today. ☞

SUPPORTING EVIDENCE:
5 MORE DARK EXCURSIONS INTO FILM NOIR

1. *Detour* (1945, USA; Edgar G. Ulmer, dir.)
An utterly hopeless sad sack heads to California to meet up with his girl; along the way, he hooks up with a snarling femme fatale and finds himself drawn into a downward spiral of fear and death. This low-budget Poverty Row production is film noir stripped down to its most raw, potent elements.

2. *The Postman Always Rings Twice* (1946, USA; Tay Garnett, dir.)

Stranger in town, loveless marriage, rich husband, seductive wife—there is no more essential plot setup in film noir than this one, and here it finds one of its finest expressions. James M. Cain, along with Dashiell Hammett and Raymond Chandler, was one of the era's great hard-boiled writers, and this is the best adaptation of his work.

3. *Night and the City* (1950, UK; Jules Dassin, dir.)

Exiled from Hollywood during the communist witch hunt era, director Jules Dassin emerged in England to direct this moody, cynical, uncompromising film noir. Richard Widmark turns in the performance of a lifetime as a two-bit hustler whose overreaching ambition leads to doom.

4. *The Phenix City Story* (1955, USA; Phil Karlson, dir.)

Directed by Phil Karlson, one of the most underrated filmmakers of the noir era, this fact-based drama finds a solitary crusader standing up to crime, corruption, and cynicism in an Alabama town run by the mob. A pseudo-documentary approach and a tremendously energetic and violent atmosphere make it unique.

5. *Touch of Evil* (1958, USA; Orson Welles, dir.)

Visually stunning, stylistically daring, and with a powerful story at its center, ***Touch of Evil*** finds the heart of darkness in murder and Mexican drug gangs. It's fitting that Orson Welles' return to Hollywood would find him helming one of the last great films of the noir era.

Noir is not, on its surface, a huge influence on the world of *The Sopranos*. For all their evil deeds, Tony and his men live in the light, and they are part of something bigger than themselves, unlike the lonely losers and desperate last-chancers of film noir. Ultimately, they may be as doomed as any character in the bleak world of postwar crime drama, but they're not fatalistic about it; even in the final frames of the last episode, Tony's mood is more distracted than desperate. He and his crew strive for and even achieve success; they battle law enforcement with paperwork and legal maneuvering, not with gunfire. They have different relationships with their women and with each other. (It's actually a bit dismaying how disempowered the women of *The Sopranos* seem compared with the ruthless, seductive femme fatales of noir.) Their fate may be preordained, but it triggers as much reckless optimism as it does existential despair. But where noir does have a nearly inestimable impact on *The Sopranos* is in the approach the filmmakers took to their material. A desire to press the limitations of the genre, and to fight against the restrictions imposed on it regarding the portrayal of sex, violence, and social issues, suffuses the work of David Chase and his staff.

Noir was, obviously, dark. Though usually thought of as an American creation, many of its directors and cinematographers were from the European tradition, and noir's distinctive look is something they brought with them. German expressionism, with its deep, stark shadows and sudden shafts of light; Italian neorealism, with its simple black-and-white compositions and ability to integrate characters into their surroundings, by making the settings distinct and unforgettable; French romanticism, with its cloudy mystery and swirling sense of disorientation—all these contributed to the unforgettable visual vocabulary of the best noir films. Noir was also heavily influenced by the pulp detective writers of the '30s and '40s. It was these writers, many of whom wrote for the influential *Black Mask* magazine, who introduced the colorful, snappy patter in which noir characters spoke. Their gaudy and uniquely American speech, with its outrageous images and rapid-fire, aggressively clever dialogue, was the furthest thing from realistic—and yet, coming from the mouths of the toughs, losers, and femme fatales who made up the noir universe, it seemed like the most natural thing in the world.

Those characters were another key element of noir. The genre's most productive days were in the late 1940s and early 1950s, when a generation of men were returning from a war that had shown them unbelievable horror, death, and madness. Many were physically shattered, and many more were mental wrecks. They saw and did things during the war that exposed them to the darkest corners of human activity, and often as not returned home to find that they couldn't relate to the world anymore; it had moved on without them. Many turned to crime—as an outlet for aggression, a means of coping with their sense of detachment, or just to make money—

but they did so with a sense of cynicism and alienation that set them apart from their predecessors. Film noir reflected this in a hugely arresting way: its criminals weren't mere psychopaths, nor were they bad eggs looking for an easy payoff. They were doom-struck, fatalistic, existentialist—cynical men, profoundly aware of their own insignificance, but determined to be noticed; ready to accept their own demise, but willing to take anyone out with them. Noir was littered with femme fatales, lost souls, and cocky jerks on their way to the grave. Their lives didn't matter even to themselves, and they knew it.

While these qualities might not be immediately obvious as setting a precedent for *The Sopranos*, what happened behind the camera was far clearer. Film noir arose at a time when the motion picture industry was not only still laboring under the oppression of the Hays Code, but also had to deal with a rising tide of anti-communist sentiment, which brought its own pressures to bear on filmmakers. The generation returned from the Second World War were as cynical as their fictional counterparts—they'd seen things that made it seem ridiculous to waste time on something as mean-ingless as censoring movies. The filmmakers, too—many of whom were European or American liberals, which made them susceptible to accusations of communist sympathy—wanted to tell more rel-evant, adult stories, stories of working men, of desperate criminals, of sex and violence and drugs, and they found it appalling that the desire to make movies for grown-ups was suddenly considered a disloyal act.

Film noir gave them the ability to push back, for a number of reasons. For one thing, this wave of crime dramas didn't often con-sist of big-budget blockbusters with well-known stars. They were studio films of low priority, made on the cheap with a stable of contract players instead of the era's marquee names. Many great noir films were B pictures, tagged on at the end of a double or triple feature, which made them more likely to escape the notice of the censors. They also came out of the struggling independent studios, the "Poverty Row" filmmakers who could get away with more than Warner Brothers. And the writers and directors of noir films, many of whom were quite practiced at avoiding censors in other contexts, became equally adept at skirting the requirements of the Hays Code through technicalities. Their movies were saturated with sex rendered in code words, violence delivered by implication, and adult ideas communicated to the audience with a quick wink that could slip right past the guardians of moral rectitude. Film noir thus represented some of the earliest stirrings against the establishment; it introduced, however subtly, some of the genuinely subversive elements of filmmaking that wouldn't fully bloom until the '60s and '70s.

It is difficult to pick just one movie as an exemplar of the glory days of film noir. There are simply too many great movies, each with their own admirable qualities, to make selecting a single representative of the genre an easy task. But crime films are all about tough decisions, so let us bite the bullet and make one. Joseph H. Lewis' *The Big Combo* came relatively late in the noir game—it wasn't released until 1955—and was no one's idea of a major success. It is a film, however, that holds many surprising rewards.

A slick blend of film noir and gangster picture, *The Big Combo* focuses on the clash between mob moneyman Mr. Brown (Richard Conte) and police detective Leonard Diamond (Cornel Wilde). Their relationship is more savage and personal than most; part of that stems from Brown's seeming immunity to prosecution. Since he merely serves as the bank for dozens of violent criminal enterprises, he never gets near the scene of an actual crime, and can never be tied to any wrongdoing.

But as Diamond's boss sees all too clearly, there's more to it than that. Diamond is in love with Brown's moll, a stunning, druggy blonde named Susan Lowell (played by Jean Wallace, who was Wilde's wife at the time); he also has his own girl, a dancer he treats like a spare tire while he futilely tries to get at Brown through Susan. It's an ugly situation, one that leads to Diamond eventually pursuing the case at his own expense, chasing down any lead, from a long-lost witness to a half-forgotten name, if it gets him closer to bringing down Brown.

You can't blame Diamond for wanting to rid the world of

Brown. *The Big Combo*, like *The Sopranos*, makes it pretty clear that cops and criminals are often playing a painfully similar game—but Tony, though he holds the feds in contempt, perceives himself as the victim of their disrespectful harassment. Brown, on the other hand, is nobody's victim and clearly in charge of his relationships. He rules his goons, the ambiguously homosexual Mingo and Fante, through terror. He rules his second-in-command, former big shot Joe McClure, through abuse and bullying. He rules his girlfriend with a combination of money and sex (in a scene that was notorious at the time, Brown romances her before dropping out of frame, suggesting none too lightly that she'd be his evening meal). And he rules Diamond through utter contempt. Mr. Brown is supremely confident and supremely cruel. He brutalizes one of his prizefighters for not having a killer instinct, barking that "First is first and second is nobody!" Diamond he treats with sheer dismissive scorn. He ridicules the detective's pitiful salary, mocks his legal impotence, and belittles his desire for Susan. It's a fantastic performance, and anyone who's seen it understands the easy menace Conte commands when he shows up nearly twenty years later in *The Godfather*.

The ways *The Big Combo* kicks at the restraints of the Hays Code are obvious today and must have seemed no less so at the time. It is a movie suffused with raw sexuality—the suggestive scenes with Mingo and Fante are one thing, but the relationship between Brown and Susan is quite another. It had to be filmed with the jealous Wilde away from the set (he was reportedly outraged when he saw the finished film), and it got Lewis called on the carpet by the Production Code enforcers. He responded to their endless grilling, about a scene where Brown seduces Susan in front of a table full of ill-gotten cash, with sheer resistance, refusing to admit he'd intended to imply anything racy. (When asked where Conte is supposed to have gone when he drops below camera level, Lewis shrugged and answered, "How the hell do I know?") The scene, which plays out in front of Brown's illegal "bank," also predicts the moral quandary in which women characters like Carmela Soprano would find themselves: driven to despair, but unable to leave the comfort of the gilded cage. Even the scenes of violence, including one where

Brown and his gang try to come up with a way to torture Diamond that won't leave a mark, suggest the clever ways Lewis was trying to skirt the Code.

The film has many more virtues. Its raucous, jazzy score (by David Raksin) is perfect, and its innovative cinematography—the work of the brilliant John Alton, one of noir's great stylists—is one of the reasons for its strong reputation among modern critics. Alton uses creative lighting everywhere, from single sources and at odd angles, to draw the eye, create powerful compositions, and drive home the mood in every scene. The final scene, which uses a moving spotlight to recall the famous conclusion of *Casablanca*, is justifiably praised; an early one, using a high-angled light to capture Mingo and Fante as they track down a fleeing Susan, divides her figure at the line of her *décolletage* and makes her look naked and vulnerable. Lewis' direction is wonderful, the equal of his other noir classic, *Gun Crazy*, and screenwriter Philip Yordan, known for his rapid-fire scripts, doesn't disappoint here. As a predictor of the themes that noir would bestow on *The Sopranos*, *The Big Combo* is a success; as an archetype of noir itself, it's a small masterpiece.

THIS GUN FOR HIRE AND WARTIME NOIR

Film noir's appeal was multifaceted, but few could deny that much of it came from its status as a point of resistance against the restrictions of the Hays Code. The creators of noir constantly bristled at restrictions on morality, violence, and sexual behavior, and much of this began in the wartime era. With millions dying in remote corners of the globe, it seemed increasingly absurd to impose such standards on portraying corruption and brutality in cinema. One of the first to slough off the standards of the censors was the decidedly unsentimental Graham Greene, who had already created a memorable noir villain in *Brighton Rock*'s sadistic spoiled Catholic, Pinkie Brown. Greene also penned the original story that formed the basis of 1942's brutal *This Gun for Hire*.

One of the central conflicts in *The Sopranos*, informing everything from Tony's splintered self-image to Carmela's conflicts over her status and wealth, is the simple fact that the heart of the gangster's success rests on pure, bloody violence. It forces us to contemplate the fact that there are people in the world who make their living at murder. The inner life of a killer—how such people operate, how they reconcile their slaughter with a presumed self-conception as decent, who pays them to do such awful things—is the subject not just of *The Sopranos*, but of *This Gun for Hire*, one of the best of the wartime noirs. (For an even darker, more nihilistic take on the same subject, see 1961's eerie, bleak *Blast of Silence*.)

Alan Ladd plays Raven, a sharp-faced and incredibly determined professional killer. Hired to murder a corporate blackmailer, Raven is cheated by his employer, a chemical company flunky played by Laird Cregar, who pays him off in marked bills, hoping the hit man will be caught and executed. Raven finds out and swears revenge, and throughout the course of a movie crammed with plot angles and twisted relationships, his tunnel vision and obsessive determination prove why the worst thing you can do is cross a killer. Along the way, he reveals a history of childhood trauma that shaped him into the remorseless death-dealer he eventually became—an early cinematic attempt to provide a psychological background for a criminal's behavior.

There are plenty of other elements at work in *This Gun for Hire*. The romance between a singer and police detective (Veronica Lake and Robert Preston) is pretty charming, a wartime profiteering plot works as a historical curio, and the hulking Cregar plays Ladd's double-crossing employer as a perfectly oily coward. But the center of the story, and the aspect that will resonate with fans of *The Sopranos*, is its treatment of the savage, determined Raven, single-minded and calculating, his past flecked with blood and his psyche irredeemably twisted from an early age. It's people like him who keep Tony Soprano and his family in new furniture and nights out at fancy restaurants; it's the deaths they cause that keep his empire running. And David Chase rarely lets us forget it.

THE DARK PAST AND THE ARRIVAL OF PSYCHOLOGY

Psychological theory isn't a new approach in the ages-old attempt to understand the compulsion toward crime. As long as there have been criminals, there have been people who tried to figure out why they committed their wicked deeds. From the precepts of the early church stating that crime was a sickness of the soul all the way through nineteenth-century belief in phrenology, experts and laymen alike have advanced all sorts of theories about what the criminal mind is made of. But the early days of the twentieth century, after the theories of Sigmund Freud made the inner urges of the ego and the id part of our shared vocabulary, brought the study of the mind to the forefront of all the arts. Just as *The Sopranos* began with Dr. Melfi thinking her psychological insights could help Tony get on the straight and narrow, and ended with her believing he was just using therapy as a means of becoming a more perfect criminal, psychology in crime films has followed a long and disturbing arc.

The 1948 film noir *The Dark Past* didn't see much of a release when it first debuted; directed by B movie specialist Rudolph Maté, it played to small audiences and even today is hard to find on video. But it marked a key moment in the career of one of its stars, and was one of the earliest crime dramas to make psychology a central element of its plot.

Psychoanalysis still wasn't taken seriously by much of the general public, and generally thought of as a dodge or a type of quackery—a belief reflected in the plot of *The Dark Past*. At its outset, Lee J. Cobb, playing a police psychiatrist, encounters resistance from a detective when he suggests a young hood might benefit from psychoanalysis. To convince the detective, Cobb tells the story of how he once overcame a maniacal killer who had taken a family hostage by talking the criminal through the dark shadows of his own mind.

Cobb is outstanding as the psychiatrist, but the real standout is William Holden as the killer. Holden had previously been known for playing handsome but bland leading man roles; the character of Al Walker opened up new opportunities for him and helped shape him into one of the most respected actors of the postwar era. Nina Foch is also excellent as Walker's moll, trapped between his psychopathic behavior and Cobb's manipulation.

In addition to being an early attempt to introduce audiences to the idea that a criminal's behavior might be rooted in childhood influences and that early trauma might be responsible for sociopathic tendencies later in life, *The Dark Past* features another critical aspect that would ripple into the future and inform *The Sopranos*: Al Walker, it turns out, is haunted by a recurring and violent dream that holds the secret to his adult maladjustment. David Chase may not have seen the film, but some of its ideas wound up paying off in his creation.

STERLING HAYDEN, THE ESSENTIAL ANTIHERO

For most actors in noir, crime dramas, and gangster films, moviemaking is a means of escape, a way of indulging in the fantasy of a dangerous life with the knowledge that, when the cameras go off for the day, everything will be safe and secure again. (Although with a few of *The Sopranos*' performers, the line between real life and fiction blurred, and they discovered the law was not quite as ineffectual as it was portrayed on the show. A number of cast members, including Lillo Brancato Jr., Robert Iler, Tony Darrow, and Richard Maldone, were arrested for Mafia-style crimes both during and after the show's run.) But that wasn't the case with Sterling Hayden, the imposing actor who starred in some of the best crime movies of the 1950s. The tough characters he played were practically kittens compared with who he was in real life; far from a petty thug, Hayden was a genuine war hero who risked his life smuggling weapons to anti-Nazi partisans and carrying out sabotage missions behind enemy lines.

Born in 1916 in New Jersey, Hayden dropped out of school at sixteen and began the life of a sailor, captaining a ship from Massachusetts to Tahiti by the time he was twenty-two. After doing some modeling, the ruggedly handsome, towering young man signed to Paramount, who marketed his good looks by dubbing him "the most beautiful man in the movies." He bristled under this reputation—he wanted to be judged on his talent—and quit to join the Marines after making only two movies. When the Second World War broke out, Hayden served with distinction and heroism, earning a Silver Star.

When he returned, he began to make gritty, raw films that took advantage of his fearsome demeanor and his easy, cool sense of danger, rather than his attractiveness. Some of his greatest roles included cunning heavy Dix Handley in the classic heist film *The Asphalt Jungle*, retired gunslinger Johnny Guitar in Nicholas Ray's psycho-western of the same name, and ultra-efficient criminal mastermind Johnny Clay in Stanley Kubrick's 1956 noir *The Killing*. All these roles showcased him as a prototypical antihero—though the characters were all hoodlums with shady pasts and criminal tendencies, they had their own moral codes that made audiences like them in spite of those darker qualities.

Even having found new success in Hollywood, Hayden was still his own man; like his characters, he refused to live by anyone else's rules. When the lifestyle of a celebrity began to wear on him, he simply left: he sailed around the world, spent time with his children, and in 1963 published the fascinating memoir *Wanderer*, in which he boldly rejected the materialistic trappings of modern American life and reveled in the freedom to live as he chose. He didn't make another movie for eight years, but when he returned, he proved he still had plenty to offer: he turned in memorable roles as the mad General Ripper in *Dr. Strangelove*, Roger Wade in the 1973 version of Raymond Chandler's *The Long Goodbye*, and, most critically for fans of *The Sopranos*, the crooked cop McCluskey in *The Godfather*. Throughout his career, Hayden played men like himself—bold men who turned their bristling personalities to their advantage—and lived a life almost free of compromise in an industry that frowns on individuality.

THE THIRD MAN AND POSTWAR PROFITEERING

Long before the directors of the French New Wave, besotted with a romantic view of the American crime drama, made movies like *Pickpocket* and *Breathless*, a collection of major talents came together to make a markedly more cynical postwar noir. Written by English novelist Graham Greene (the mind behind *Brighton Rock* and *This Gun for Hire*), directed by his countryman Carol Reed, and set in Vienna during its post-WWII occupation by four Allied powers, 1949's *The Third Man* is a terrifically moody crime drama that deftly juggles light humor with bleak emotional moments.

The story follows Holly Martins, a pulp novelist in dire financial straits played by Joseph Cotten. Martins accepts an offer to visit his old friend Harry Lime (Orson Welles) in Vienna, only to learn on arrival that Lime has been killed in a freak accident. A British policeman informs him that Lime was a crook and a swindler, but Martins won't believe it—he sees the affair through the eyes of a mystery writer. He learns from friends (and Lime's ex-lover, played by the hopelessly devoted Alida Valli) that his old chum really *was* a criminal—and might not be dead after all. Cotten's measured, quietly desperate performance reflects the painful moral ambivalence of a man who is torn between the law, which insists he help bring Lime to justice, and a woman begging him to let the same man go free.

The Third Man is now considered an all-time noir classic and a key link between the European art film and the American crime drama. It's also a must-see for fans of *The Sopranos* for a number of reasons. Just as Tony Soprano somehow seizes viewer sympathy while indulging in endless immoral exploits, it is impossible to resist the easy charisma of Welles' Harry Lime as he sneeringly profits off of the misery of the desperate population of postwar Austria. In one of the film's most famous scenes, Lime takes Martins up on a Ferris wheel that could just as easily be on the Jersey shore and looks down at the people far below. "Look down there," he says. "Tell me, would you really feel any pity of one of those dots stopped moving forever? If I offered you twenty thousand pounds for every dot that stopped, would you really, old man, tell me to keep my money, or would you calculate how many dots you could afford to spare?"

It is impossible not to draw parallels between the hulking Tony Soprano, forever in denial about the human costs of his profession, and the calculating Harry Lime, breezily dismissing the moral viciousness of his enterprise. And in the relationship between Martins and Valli's character, we see reflections of the frustrations of Father Phil, who can't understand the emotional and social bonds that cause Carmela to stay loyal to Tony, even though the price might be her soul. Finally, just as Tony became an antihero in spite of himself, so too did Harry Lime, who lived on in radio as a sort of roguish adventurer.

PSYCHO AND THE DECLINE OF NOIR

When it came to crime films, master of suspense Alfred Hitchcock was both of them and above them. While he shared some of the concerns of classic noir (distrust of the police, lurid violence, and flashy on-screen compositions), he had little interest in the bleakness and despair of the low-budget postwar crime dramas. He believed in the idea of the innocent man (even if he frequently put that man through the wringer); he generally eschewed shadowy black-and-white for dazzling color; and he showed little interest in the inner workings of gangsters or criminal syndicates, preferring to use spies and sociopaths to provide an element of danger to his stories. And while he worked from stories by some legendary crime writers (especially Cornell Woolrich, for *Rear Window*, and the French team of Boileau-Narcejac, for *Vertigo*), few of Hitchcock's films are considered noir or gangster films in the classic sense.

But although he exercised a minimal influence on crime drama while it thrived, Hitchcock arguably played a major role in its demise. With the release of his masterpiece *Psycho* in 1960—his last truly great picture—he not only achieved huge commercial and critical success, but also plunged a dagger into the heart of the traditional crime film, dealing it a near-lethal blow from which it would only have partially recovered by the time *The Sopranos* debuted. Hitchcock was nearly as great a showman as he was a director, and his marketing of *Psycho* turned it into a smash hit, which meant that its villain—the unstable hotelier Norman Bates (Anthony Perkins)—would represent a new kind of movie criminal, one who would steer movies into an entirely different direction for the next four decades.

Norman Bates had a domineering mother similar to Tony Soprano's, but found a more direct way of dealing with her. While the criminals and killers in classic crime and gangster films had been unsavory, they had at least been relatable—we could understand them, if not forgive them. Their motives, no matter how vast their cruelty, were comprehensible: they wanted money, power, and respect.

In the wake of *Psycho*, more and more movie villains became maniacs, sociopaths, and lunatics—we might have some empathy with their madness, but what drove them was entirely mysterious. Since we could not understand them, we found it easier to punish them. As social morality grew more ambiguous, our film villains became more starkly evil, just as the noir period had brought us more morally complex villains in a more socially conservative time. From the '60s all through the '80s, with few exceptions, crime films began to glorify the police and portray criminals as inhuman psychopaths, culminating in the slasher flicks of the 1980s. It was a scenario Hitchcock himself—who thought little of law enforcement and clearly didn't give much credence to Norman Bates' motivations—never would have anticipated, but the role he played in it is undeniable. Noir was as dead as Marion Crane, and a generation of Norman Bateses would follow.

Warren Beatty and Faye Dunaway in *Bonnie and Clyde*. (Warner Bros. Pictures/Photofest)

3

I'M YOUR FAMILY:
THE CHANGING FACE OF CRIME

BONNIE AND CLYDE

With the advent of color, the decline of noir, and the intro-duction of the new-model villain, crime movies began to hit the doldrums in the early 1960s. The French New Wave had electrified cinema, and its use of daring new techniques combined with classic elements of crime drama raised the bar for directors all over the world. But it wasn't just changes in cinematic style that led to this wandering in the wilderness; there was something new in the air socially. A whole new generation of educated young people was beginning to emerge. Their tastes were more sophisticated, their behavior was more daring, and their political views were decidedly different from those of their parents. And most of all, they had money. Movies of the film noir era had pushed back against the strictures of the Production Code; the new generation wanted it shattered. They were looking for an entirely new approach to the crime drama. In 1967, Arthur Penn would give them what they were looking for—in spades.

The movie that would become *Bonnie and Clyde*, one of the first successful products from a new generation of maverick Hollywood filmmakers and a film that forever changed the crime drama, was a troubled production from the start. Warner Brothers executives originally conceived it as a comedic, almost campy take on the classic gangster film, but were dissatisfied with the controversial material in early drafts of the script. Eventually coming to think of the project as a lost cause, they decided to bury it as a B picture with a limited release, and to save money by offering Warren Beatty—the film's producer as well as its star—a large percentage of its profits rather than a high salary. They reckoned it a safe bet, since they didn't expect it to collect any profits. With the French New Wave turning heads all over the world, François Truffaut and Jean-Luc Godard were both considered for the directing job, but the former had a scheduling conflict and the latter was ultimately deemed too much of a risk, because of the unconventional nature of his films.

Arthur Penn was finally brought on, and he proved to be a perfect choice. His previous two films had been *Mickey One*, a bizarrely stylized film noir heavily influenced by the nouvelle vague, and *The Chase*, a socially relevant picture about racism and discrimination in the South. In conjunction with his writers (David Newman, Robert Benton, and Robert Towne), he applied many of the filmmaking techniques of the New Wave to his work, and added his own bold sense of energy, as well as a willingness to defy restrictions about sexuality and violence that young audiences had been bristling at for years. Picking Penn was just the right move. Teens and twenty-somethings crammed the theaters and made *Bonnie and Clyde* into one of the biggest hits in the studio's history. It was they who made a millionaire out of Warren Beatty and his joke of a contract; it was they who felt that the brutality and cruelty of Vietnam made a joke of the Hays Code and its finger-wagging moralism, and who presided over its final destruction to open up a new era of filmmaking in which frank sexuality and bloody violence were now allowed to appear on screen.

Unsurprisingly, *Bonnie and Clyde* was as controversial as it was successful, and much of the divergence played out along generational lines. Older people found the glorification of a pair of heartless killers as outrageous as it had been in the 1930s; younger people focused on the pair's doomed romance and inability to get by in the "straight" world. Conservatives focused on the bad behavior of the title characters; liberals pointed out the harm done to them by the authorities. The World War II generation found the violence and sexual content arbitrary and offensive; their children saw a reaction to the horrors of Vietnam and the hypocrisy of the moral scolds in power. The divide played out among professional film critics: *The New York Times'* veteran reviewer Bosley Crowther penned a vituperative critique of the film that got him fired for seeming out of step with the kids who'd made *Bonnie and Clyde* a smash, while the younger Pauline Kael leveraged her love of the film into a staff job at *The New Yorker*. Not even the marketing campaign escaped unscathed. The film's original tagline was the chilling "They're young . . . they're in love . . . and they kill people." This proved altogether too nihilistic for the studio, and even as *Bonnie and Clyde* was making money hand over fist, it was changed to "They're young. They're in love. They rob banks."

Even those who have never seen *Bonnie and Clyde* should be familiar with the story. It is *Romeo and Juliet* with tommy guns, the tragic story of a young couple in the throes of a doomed love, drawn from the real lives of two of the most notorious Depression-era gangsters. Clyde Barrow and Bonnie Parker (Beatty and Faye Dunaway) meet cute in Depression-era Texas, and soon, having met with both assistance and opposition from their families, are tearing through America, raising hell and robbing gas stations. Theirs is not the utterance of transcendent love under the branches, but the raw sexual language of the gun; more than a few critics have noted the similarities between this film, when Clyde first produces his revolver to have its barrel lovingly stroked by Bonnie, and Joseph H. Lewis' similarly overheated doomed-romance noir *Gun Crazy*. Like *Romeo and Juliet*, the two young lovers have no chance, and will be gone be the time the story ends; but unlike Shakespeare's characters' genteel expirations, Bonnie and Clyde go out in fountains of blood, providing the movie with an unforgettable ending and forever changing the rules about what level of violence was acceptable in a crime film.

This may be *Bonnie and Clyde*'s greatest gift to *The Sopranos*. The way it broke taboos about sex (Dunaway appears in the film's first scene almost totally nude, literally bashing away at her tiny room—a reflection of the trap she feels her life has become—and within minutes, the movie breaches the topics of impotence and homosexuality) and violence set the tone for more latitude in movies and eventually television, and helped David Chase tell the story he wanted to tell. It also made a case for the careful integration of music into narrative, making a hit out of Lester Flatt and Earl Scruggs' decades-old "Foggy Mountain Breakdown."

On a deeper level, *Bonnie and Clyde* also introduced a psychological depth to crime stories that would echo forward all the way to the 1990s. Like Chase, Arthur Penn was able to show his characters as full of bluff and self-delusion, while still conveying sympathy for their situation and their attempt to build identities out of sheer will. There is a sense that, as with mob families, Bonnie and Clyde have created their own world with its own dynamics—as everything begins to crumble around them, he tries to keep her close by saying, "I'm your family." Family, here as in the world of *The Sopranos*, is both the greatest comfort and the deepest threat. ☞

SUPPORTING EVIDENCE: 5 MORE EXCITING DEVELOPMENTS FROM TURBULENT TIMES

1. *Pale Flower* (1964, JAP; Masahiro Shinoda, dir.)

Seijun Suzuki is primarily responsible for the high esteem in which Japanese yakuza films of the '60s are held, but *Pale Flower* proves his wasn't the only game in town. A riveting story of a mob killer newly released from prison who forms an alliance with a beautiful young woman addicted to high-stakes thrills, it is a suspenseful and psychologically fascinating film.

2. *Topkapi* (1964, USA; Jules Dassin, dir.)

The ever-versatile Jules Dassin, who had proven a master of film noir and one of the pioneers of the French heist film, was just as adept at transferring his skills to the caper movie. This romping international adventure featured an all-star collection of criminal specialists and won Peter Ustinov an Oscar for his role as the gang's would-be fall guy.

3. *Point Blank* (1967, USA; John Boorman, dir.)

Adapted from a classic pulp novel by Donald Westlake, *Point Blank* neatly dovetails a noir sensibility and French New Wave techniques into a gangland revenge thriller. Lee Marvin is grimly powerful as the thief whose betrayal sets up a relentless, bloody reprisal.

4. Madigan (1968, USA; Don Siegel, dir.)

A tight, tense police action thriller penned by two blacklisted screenwriters and directed by the man who would go on to form a legendary collaboration with Clint Eastwood, *Madigan* was an excellent example of the '60s police procedural. It would have a powerful reach on television (it even became a series itself) and helped establish the crime film archetype of the freewheeling cop who frequently strays outside the system.

5. Violent City (1970, ITA; Sergio Sollima, dir.)

One of the new developments in crime drama that stood out during this period was the *poliziotteschi*, a strain of high-octane, action-packed, violent mob thrillers that emerged in the late 1960s and early 1970s. *Violent City* was unusual for the type—it featured American actors (Charles Bronson played the lead role of a betrayed assassin), was set in New Orleans, and was directed by a filmmaker who specialized in westerns—but it was also a huge success in Italy and helped launch the genre.

Both Penn and Chase are firmly in control of their characters' moral presentation, but they are wise enough to give viewers plenty of room for interpretation. David Chase held his Mafia family in low moral esteem, and at times he almost went out of his way to remind viewers that they should feel guilty rooting for a man of such base character. (He seemed particularly frustrated at the reaction of fans after the final episode.) But he knew well enough that he had to present Tony and the rest of his gang in just the right light—never letting viewers forget the mobsters' inherent bad nature, but keeping them interested enough to tune in week after week. Penn and his writers toed a similar line: while the movie became a huge hit thanks to the young people who embraced Bonnie and Clyde as rebel antiheroes, their pathology is far darker than simple youthful defiance.

Bonnie Parker and Clyde Barrow were just kids, in the strictest sense: they had only the barest conception of themselves as people, and—just like the rebellious teen girls who donned berets after seeing Faye Dunaway wear one—were forming a sense of their own identities based on what they saw in the newspapers. The Barrow gang largely copycatted the other public enemies on J. Edgar Hoover's list. Many of their robberies were penny-ante service station and grocery stories, but they were still aping their betters, with Clyde and his brother studying the moves of John Dillinger. Bonnie expressed herself through simplistic poetry, and posed for photographs she knew would be on the front pages of newspapers; Clyde was impotent, but clung to his relationship with Bonnie because of the status he felt it conferred on him as the gang's leader. When Clyde is attacked by a grocer whose store he is looting, he expresses real shock—he's built up an image in his mind of himself as a defender of the working man against the banks and big shots, and can't fathom why he'd be assaulted by someone trying to save his meager business in the depths of a depression. The kids who filled the theatres in 1967 and the people who tuned in to HBO in 1999 may both have missed the point, but watching *Bonnie and Clyde* and *The Sopranos* in close succession, it couldn't be clearer. These are deeply damaged people who build their lives around a fiction that makes it possible for them to live.

Much has been made of the historical accuracy of *Bonnie and Clyde*, and it's true that it takes many liberties with the facts. But Penn was never trying to make a historical biography of two Depression-era criminals, any more than Chase was trying to launch an investigation of the Mafia in its late stages. Arthur Penn was trying to make a story about a self-created American myth, and to do so, he had to dispense with the facts and give the story room to breathe. If he cut corners with the historical facts, it wasn't that different from what J. Edgar Hoover himself did, ignoring the poison of organized crime while elevating the likes of Barrow and Parker to the status of gorgons. If Bonnie's poem, recited in the film just before her gruesome demise, is nothing but self-aggrandizing doggerel to justify the crimes she and her man had committed, she still wasn't wrong in thinking that the law had no interest in trying them, but simply wanted to shoot them down like dogs. (Famously, when Alvin "Creepy" Karpis, the last of the public enemies, was captured, he had to be bound with a necktie. No one had bothered to bring handcuffs, since it was assumed he'd just be gunned down like his predecessors.) The public played its part, too, eating up salacious newspaper articles that rarely failed to mention that the Barrow gang was made up of two young and attractive couples. Complaints about its historical accuracy would plague *Bonnie and Clyde* in other ways, as well: no fewer than two lawsuits were filed by people unhappy with their depictions, or the depictions of their kin, in the film. That is one reason so many subsequent movies have shied away from using the real names of people whose crimes are depicted on screen.

Its correspondence to the historical record aside, *Bonnie and Clyde* has remained a lasting classic. Its sex may no longer seem as frank, and its violence may no longer seem as bloody, but the impact it had in 1967 can't be overestimated, and every step forward made in the subsequent decade was along a trail it had blazed. The '70s would see much progress in the breadth and depth of the crime drama, and it would be a key decade for the films that laid the groundwork for *The Sopranos*. None of it would have been possible if not for Arthur Penn and his Romeo and Juliet of crime.

LE DEUXIÈME SOUFFLE AND FRENCH HEIST FILMS

Though American and European crime films fed off one another and influenced each other over the decades, there have always been certain distinctions. There are always exceptions, but as a rule, American crime dramas have concerned themselves with plot and idea, while their European counterparts are more interested in style and tone. And in a reflection of differing social and legal systems, America's criminals, both on screen and in the real world, are far more prone toward violence and the easy death coming from the barrel of a gun than are their European cousins.

At least partly due to lack of easy access to firearms and the more severe penalties for their use, many real-life European gangs kept bloodshed to a minimum and relied on clever planning and complex schemes for their criminal paydays. This is reflected in the European approach to crime drama: while American gangster movies showed their kingpins ruling by the strength of the tommy gun, French films developed along different lines, with the "heist film" becoming a showcase for many talented directors. The heist film was cinematically effective, because it allowed for complex plots where intelligence trumped force and success depended on perfect planning instead of mere brutality. It also required the assembly of a team of experts, which allowed directors and screenwriters to populate their films with all sorts of colorful characters, providing inspiration for talented actors. Heist films were made in America as well, but the French seemed to have a particular genius for them.

French directors in the '50s and '60s produced one classic after another in the heist movie mold, influenced by both American film noir and the bourgeoning European art film movement. Jean-Luc Godard's New Wave classic *Bande à Part*, Jules Dassin's early French noir classic *Du Rififi Chez les Hommes*, and Claude Lelouch's flashy 1970 film *Le Voyou* are all fine examples of the type, but the undisputed master of the French heist film was Jean-Pierre Melville. He virtually launched the genre with 1956's riveting, stylish *Bob le Flambeur* and followed it up with such films as 1967's *Le Samouraï*, featuring an early iteration of the existential hit man archetype, and 1970's fascinating *Le Cercle Rouge*. But his quintessential work in the heist vein is 1966's *Le Deuxième Souffle* (*The Second Breath*).

A classic so stylish and solid it is hard to look away from, *Le Deuxième Souffle* features everything a great heist picture should have: a cool, calculating mastermind (Lino Ventura); a relentless police detective (wonderfully played by Paul Meurisse); a career criminal looking for one last score; a beautiful woman (Christine Fabréga) in a dangerous situation; and double crosses and betrayals lurking around every corner. The world of *The Sopranos* leaned heavily on the American style of violence and extortion as the means to illicit wealth, but some of the more elaborate jobs hatched by Tony's crew—themselves informed by *GoodFellas*, whose plot is driven by two high-profile real-world heists—echo *The Sopranos*' Old World forebears.

OCEAN'S ELEVEN
AND HOW HEISTS BECAME CAPERS

Just as American gangster pictures subtly transformed into heist movies during their journey across the Atlantic to Europe, heist movies themselves underwent a transformation when they were shipped back to the U.S. Europe's less violent, not so heavily armed culture affected the way crime was portrayed on screen, and this reflected reality gave American filmmakers license to portray a kinder, gentler kind of organized crime. Filmmakers and audiences alike reckoned that, denatured of the cruelty and bloodshed that marked their real-world counterparts, criminals weren't so bad after all. Thus followed a number of movies where the on-screen gangs were more lovable rogues than violent thugs, and the caper film was born. Even the name indicated this essential difference: a heist was unmistakably a criminal enterprise, while a caper carried the implication of play.

Frank Sinatra—a man who deliberately courted the friendship of genuine Mafia figures—turned out to be a key figure in the establishment of the caper movie. Though quite popular with his fans, 1960's *Ocean's Eleven* wasn't exactly a great film; it was, like many of the so-called "Rat Pack" movies, more or less an excuse for him to hang out with his celebrity buddies and screw around in his favorite Las Vegas watering holes. But it struck a real chord with those looking for a new type of crime story and perfectly suited the easy, happy-go-lucky feel of the early 1960s, helping move audiences into a decade of flux in the cinema.

Ocean's Eleven was directed by an old Hollywood pro named Lewis Milestone, who had done crime films as early as 1928 (a pre-Code movie called *The Racket*) and was behind at least one classic film noir, 1946's *The Strange Love of Martha Ivers*. But Sinatra was a driving force behind it, playing shows on the Strip at night while filming during the day (and carrying on wild parties every free moment in between). His Rat Pack crew—including Dean Martin, Sammy Davis Jr., Peter Lawford, Joey Bishop, and Henry Silva—played the band of ex-soldiers who plan to rob five Vegas casinos on New Year's Eve. The overall lack of violence and gunplay built into the format left plenty of room for comedy to take the place of the grim sense of despair and doom that often characterized crime films.

While Sinatra and his pals clearly had a great time filming *Ocean's Eleven*, their well-lubricated camaraderie got in the way of their making a truly accomplished movie. George Clooney had better luck forty-one years later with a remake that launched a whole series; he and his co-stars may have lacked the real charisma of the Rat Pack, but they managed to deliver a slightly more professional product. *The Sopranos* was too immersed in the mob's culture of violence to fall into the caper tradition, but even aside from their idolization of Frank Sinatra, the DiMeo mob occasionally let the influence of the *Ocean's Eleven* style show in their lighter moments.

SEIJUN SUZUKI, STYLISH YAKUZA FILM AUTEUR

Largely isolated on the East Coast, Tony Soprano and his crew never encountered the Japanese organized crime outfit known as the *yakuza*. But just as the gangster film shaped the world in which Tony's family exists, the yakuza epic not only had a huge effect on Asian filmmaking, but also made criminal gangs an essential part of Japanese national culture. The yakuza have their own particular customs and traditions, but they share with the Mafia a twisted sense of honor, an almost ritualistic method of organization, and, most important, a savvy sense of their own image in the public eye.

Though the yakuza have their origins in feudal society, the conservative Japanese film industry wasn't ready to see them portrayed on the big screen right away. It wasn't until the postwar Japanese movie boom that yakuza films made their first appearances, and even then, it was with a reluctance and delicacy that would have been familiar to American moviegoers.

But in the 1960s, a rogue filmmaker named Seijun Suzuki made an indelible mark on Japanese cinema through the creation of a series of daring, unforgettable yakuza films that would influence

Asian and American cinema for decades. Like a lot of the noir filmmakers in postwar America, Suzuki emerged from the low-budget, low-standard B movie system, creating cheap and disreputable thrillers for Nikkatsu Studios. But he was also ambitious and daring, and had a flair for visual art and storytelling that reached far beyond the world of cheap films. Like many of his American peers, Suzuki worked with a set of preferred actors (his muse was a rough-and-tumble actor with a curious face, Joe Shishido), and he too often clashed with his studio bosses over what shape his movies would take. He ultimately won a lawsuit against Nikkatsu after they fired him for making the movie, *Branded to Kill*, he wanted to make, instead of the movie they expected.

Not every picture Suzuki made was in the yakuza genre (his 1966 film *Fighting Elegy*, where Christian youth gangs sublimate their sexual frustration into brawling, is particularly unforgettable), but that is where he made his greatest impact. Movies like 1963's *Youth of the Beast*, 1966's *Tokyo Drifter*, and 1967's *Branded to Kill* were ultra-stylish, gorgeous examples of the Eastern gangster genre, with beautifully composed shots, absurdly over-the-top conflicts, and boundless energy. His studio clashes led to Suzuki's decade-long blacklisting, but his movies went on to inspire an entire generation of Asian action directors, particularly Hong Kong stylists like John Woo and Wong Kar-Wai—and, through them, Western filmmakers like Quentin Tarantino. In much the same way as Tony Soprano's Mafiosi see themselves as the inheritors of both real-life mob tradition and the tradition as it's been portrayed on film, the characters in the films of Woo and Tarantino live in a world whose initial architect was Seijun Suzuki. By the time he made a triumphant comeback in 2001 with *Pistol Opera* (itself a sort of reboot of *Branded to Kill*), the world was ready to give him the glory he'd been denied during his exile.

UNDERWORLD U.S.A.'S HEADLINE REALISM

Unlike many of the police and legal procedurals that came before and after, *The Sopranos* rarely dived into the "ripped from today's headlines" approach to storytelling. In fact, episodes that stabbed at "relevance" often come across now as heavy-handed or dated. The show did, however, follow general trends in law enforcement and the mob's reaction to them, and used them as jumping-off points for dramatic narratives, such as the parallels between Junior Soprano's increasing dementia and real-life Mafioso Vincent "Chin" Gigante's feigning mental illness to dodge prosecution.

In this respect, *The Sopranos* echoed the approach of visceral, muscular moviemaker Samuel Fuller. His energetic 1961 mob noir *Underworld U.S.A.* was drawn from then-current events—specifically, articles in the *Saturday Evening Post* and other publications about Mafia activity, and the notorious 1957 crime summit in Apalachin, New York—and was intended to cash in on the public thirst for organized-crime stories. After decades of being assured by FBI boss J. Edgar Hoover that there was no such thing as organized crime, the public was growing skeptical and hungry for some mob action. However, Fuller merely used these elements as a framework to tell the story *he* wanted to tell. Few elements of the original material are even recognizable, but what *Underworld U.S.A.* sacrifices in historical accuracy, it makes up for in sheer raw power.

Cliff Robertson plays Tolly Devlin, a street hood who, like Tony Soprano, was probably doomed to a career in crime from birth. Born in prison to a convict mother who died soon after, Tolly is raised by his father—also a no-good petty crook—in the older man's own sordid footsteps. After seeing his father beaten to death in an alley, the teenage Tolly becomes a sort of Batman in reverse: he steps up his own criminal career and gets himself thrown in prison to exact a grim deathbed revenge on one of the killers. Scornful of both cops and crooks, and reliant only on a blowsy, shady bar owner played by Beatrice Kay (shades of one of *The Sopranos'* most resonant themes!), Tolly becomes a single-minded, vicious engine of vengeance, risking everything to honor a father who barely took notice of him.

Fuller has a justified reputation as the maker of effective movies that overcome their low budgets to deliver intense gut punches. (He may be best remembered for his epic war film *The Big Red One*, but his other crime dramas, especially *Pickup on South Street* and *The*

Naked Kiss, are also highly recommended.) He is ably abetted in *Underworld U.S.A.* by Harry Sukman's striking score and Hal Mohr's stark black-and-white cinematography. Alert fans of *The Sopranos* will note many elements from the movie that would later appear on the show, from the first shot (of the teenage Tolly's eyes in extreme close-up) to the kinetic fight scenes to the rows of sleazy, run-down storefronts. By using headline realism as an inspiration rather than a playbook, Fuller provided a profitable example for the movies and TV series to come.

THE BROTHERHOOD, THE FIRST REAL MAFIA MOVIE

By 1968, the time was more than ripe for a Mafia epic. Movies about organized crime had been popular and critical successes for fifty years, and the existence of the Mafia was an open secret. Serious mob wars had taken place in New York as recently as five years previous, and big heists by organized criminals were commonplace in the late '60s. The public appetite seemed primed for a major motion picture about life in *La Cosa Nostra.*

Numerous factors had kept the Mafia off the big screen. The entertainment industry, ever ready to take anyone's money, was sensitive to the possibility of offending Italian-Americans and reluctant to present movies or television shows featuring gangs of criminals made up of nothing but; the result was a succession of movies set in the world of New York organized crime, but populated with bad guys with suspiciously Anglo-Saxon surnames. J. Edgar Hoover's reluctance to admit to the existence of the Mafia helped slow things down, as well. But barriers were beginning to fall: law enforcement broke up the Apalachin Meeting, a 1957 conference of high-level Mafia bosses, and Hoover was forced to revise his public position. Just six years later, Joe Valachi, a soldier in the Genovese family, testified before a Senate subcommittee, spilling many mob secrets.

1968 saw the publication of Joe's biography, *The Valachi Papers,* and the time seemed right for a real, authentic Mafia movie. *The Brotherhood* was penned by Lewis John Carlino, an Italian-American, whose participation the studio hoped would take the sting off the film with that group. (Carlino would go on to pen other celebrated films like *The Mechanic* and *The Great Santini*.) Martin Ritt, who'd had a big success with *Hud*, signed on to direct. The movie was actually quite good. It told the story—one that would seem remarkably familiar within only a few years—of the beloved son of a Mafia don returning from the war and trying to go straight, only to find the pressures of his family's criminal traditions pulling him inexorably back in. It was also well cast, with Kirk Douglas as the tortured Mafioso and a terrific supporting performance by Susan Strasberg. The movie pulls its punches a bit (a new multi-ethnic mob has begun to supplant the Sicilian gangs from which Douglas emerged), but it's still a gripping, watchable crime drama.

Unfortunately, it was a box office disaster. It bombed in theaters, making very little money and proving—to the studio that produced it, anyway—that the public wasn't quite as ready for a Mafia movie as they'd predicted. That studio happened to be Paramount, and they swore off making mob pictures for the immediate future. Gun-shy executives wouldn't return to the genre for another four years—although when they did, they released a film with a remarkably similar premise. It would be far more successful than *The Brotherhood*, though, and would trigger a cultural revolution in crime drama and in American film. The film was *The Godfather*.

Salvatore Corsitto and Marlon Brando in *The Godfather*.
(Paramount Pictures/Photofest)

4

STRICTLY BUSINESS:
THE RISE OF THE MAFIA EPIC

THE GODFATHER

David Chase has called *GoodFellas* **the "Bible" of** *The Sopranos*. But with all due respect to the man behind the series, if *The Sopranos* can be seen as a new church of the gangster, then while *GoodFellas* may indeed be a component of scripture, it is only the New Testament. Its Old Testament, its Pentateuch, its foundational document, is *The Godfather*.

In fact, Chase was influenced by the story of Don Vito Corleone and his own troublesome family even before Francis Ford Coppola burned it into film immortality. Mario Puzo's novel of the same name, the source material for the film, seized Chase's imagination when he was in his twenties. Speaking to the Stanford University alumni magazine in 2002, he discussed his adolescent fascination with the mob: by the time Puzo's novel appeared in spring of 1969, he said, "I was just *ready* for that book." Other gangland sagas influenced Chase's greatest creation, dating all the way back to *The Public Enemy*. But no work of art had a more profound effect on *The Sopranos*, or on the characters that populated the show, than the first two *Godfather* films.

The story of Michael Corleone's tragic journey from soft-spoken young war hero who wants nothing to do with his father's criminal enterprise to blood-soaked, isolated tyrant who oversees the wholesale destruction of his family is more than an influence on *The Sopranos*. It shaped the dimensions of the entire universe in which *The Sopranos* takes place. Almost everything that happens in the show can be seen as either a continuance of, a striving for, or a reaction against what happened in Coppola's films.

It's clear as early as the first season: Tony, Paulie, Silvio, and the rest of the crew aren't just gangsters in the tradition of the Corleones. They're people who live in a world where the *Godfather* movies exist, and they pick up their cues as much from the media representations of gangster life as they do from actually living the life themselves. In some cases, as with Christopher's unmediated obsession with the movies, they almost seem to be living in a movie; Chase never engaged in any fancy winking at the fourth wall, but it was clear he meant for his Mafiosi to be as obsessed with their portrayal in the press as he was. "We did more riffing on *The Godfather*, only because I think the real wiseguys, my impression is it is more of a trip for them, only because it's a period piece and it's more operatic," he told *Vanity Fair* in 2007. "And the family was very tight. It was always our conceit that our characters would sort of learn from those films how to behave."

This tendency to view *The Godfather* and *The Godfather Part II* as a sort of ur-document, a codified statement of how a mobster is expected to behave, is present in almost every frame of *The Sopranos*, in both negative and positive ways. In the very first episode, when Tony complains that the old way of life is slipping away and that he's inherited his trade at a time when it's in decay, you cannot escape the conclusion that he's speaking of the loss of the old grandeur, the days of glittering mansions in golden Gordon Willis hues and sharp Theadora Van Runkle suits. (This is echoed by Uncle Junior's insistence on wearing tailored outfits and his bemoaning the fact that younger mobsters wear nothing but jogging suits.) Christopher idolizes Martin Scorsese. Silvio relieves tense moments with his Michael Corleone imitation. Even minor characters like rapper Massive Genius get to weigh in with an opinion that *The Godfather Part III* is "misunderstood."

There are stylistic similarities as well, not all of which can simply be chalked up to the enormous influence Coppola's films had on post-1970s cinema. More than one *Sopranos* director borrows from Coppola's directorial playbook, most especially in slow tracking shots through urban areas. The distinctive technique of switching from a high holy event to a scene of extreme criminal brutality is used repeatedly in the *Godfather* films; in *The Sopranos* it shows up as early as episode 3, when the attack on Christopher and the murder of Brendan Filone are intercut with Meadow's choir recital, where she is singing a Welsh hymn in an angelic voice. Even the legendary symbolism of the series appears early on: oranges frequently appear in the *Godfather* films as a harbinger of death, and in the first attempt on Tony's life at the end of season 1, he is caught unawares by hired hit men while holding a carton of orange juice.

But far more than this—far beyond Tony's crew's acknowledgments of Coppola's films, and beyond any simple stylistic and technical similarities—*The Godfather* and *The Sopranos* are thematically of a piece. In a way, just as Tony looks back on the lost days of glory seen in the *Godfather* films as the pinnacle of gangster triumph that he came too late to experience, *The Sopranos* is a glimpse forward to the future of the Corleone family, which Michael's ambition and single-mindedness prevent him from seeing. There are many common through-lines in the two families' stories, waiting for anyone who wants to look—though, ironically, the two family heads are generally blind to these. Which is not to say that Tony and Michael are identical; the two are far more different than they are similar. For all his talk of preserving and protecting his family, it is Michael Corleone who drives them away; the supreme irony of *The Godfather* is that Michael proves to be the pure sociopath, the calculating master of revenge even Sonny could never be. And Tony Soprano may long for the lifestyle of the Corleones, for their traditions and trappings, but brute that he is, he still cannot rival Michael for pure determined viciousness.

A more vivid through-line is found in the stories of Kay Corleone (Diane Keaton) and Carmela Soprano. Although Kay's story begins in the 1940s, she is always presented as a modern woman for her time: in touch with her emotions, strong-willed, and confrontational. She remains thus even in her Jackie O.-influenced portrayal in the maligned *Part III*; though she often flails about in an excess of helplessness, Kay is ultimately under no illusions about what her husband really is, and she risks her life and future with her children to extricate herself from his evil. In contrast, in Carmela's time, feminism has gone through multiple waves; some call the period "the postfeminist era." And yet she has largely reverted to the role prescribed for women a generation before Kay's. In temperament and in character, she's far more similar to Vito Corleone's wife. Wracked by Catholic guilt and dedicated to preserving what she perceives as traditional family roles, Carmela does suffer qualms of conscience regarding the fact that her husband is a monster. But in the end, she is far more accepting of the wealth and status that comes with being married to a high-ranking mobster than is Kay. She has far more social choices, but only seems to embrace them in a general way; her real choice is to limit herself with deliberate blindness.

Similarly, the view of mob violence as a sort of alternate form of capitalism evolves and transforms between *The Godfather* and *The Sopranos*, and it too twists into something that allows for far less possibility even though it takes place in a world of far more opportunity. In *The Godfather Part II*, Don Corleone turns to crime, as did many other immigrants of limited means, only because the normal avenues of capitalist success are not open to him, and even at the height of his power and influence, his dream for Michael is that he become a respectable member of society, a wielder of legitimate influence free from the blood and doom of ancient vendettas. His dream is a "Senator Corleone, Governor Corleone"—a genuine power who need not fear the rise of more ambitious thugs. Michael's own ambitions lie in a different direction, of course, and once he gains a taste of legitimacy, he finds it isn't so easy to extract himself from the net of crime and violence.

Contrast this with the way Tony Soprano views the straight world: to him, it's a dodge, a front, a means of hiding wealth and little else. The Corleones and the Sopranos both view the bourgeois world as hypocritical, corruptible, and imperfect, but for Vito and Michael, it is something to strive for; as perverse as its residents may be, their face of public respectability is a consummation devoutly to be desired. Tony, on the other hand, virtually seethes with contempt for his respectable neighbors. He treats his friend Davey

Scatino, whose legitimate business is jeopardized by his gambling addiction, as nothing but a mark. He barely sees the corrupt cop Vin Makazian as human until after Makazian's suicide. Outside of what advantage they can confer on him, he looks upon the non-criminal population with scorn; he refers to his neighbor Dr. Cusamano and his friends as *medigan*—slang for "American," meaning square and worthless, a "Wonder Bread wop" who buys spaghetti sauce in jars. Tony doesn't feel as if these other Italian-Americans are part of the same country, maybe not even the same race.

His perception of the family business is also at a far remove from that of his big-screen heroes. He feels no guilt that he's risen to a position of wealth committing acts of criminal violence while his childhood friend Artie Bucco had to work hard to attain modest success; he and Carmela even seem to enjoy lording it over the Buccos. Unlike Vito and his immigrant peers, Tony had full access to legitimate means of success, but found the criminal lifestyle far more rewarding, offering greater wealth and status for much less effort. He no more wants to be legitimate than he wants to join Doc Cusamano's country club, and his chief worry about his son isn't that A. J. won't be able to succeed in mainstream society, but that he doesn't have what it takes to make it as a criminal. For Tony, the straight life is something not to aspire to, but something to strenuously avoid. When Carmela urges him to cooperate with the FBI after the feds offer the family a chance to escape their life of crime and danger, he openly scoffs at the idea, mocking the notion of working for a living, selling crafts by the side of the road in New Mexico. ☞

SUPPORTING EVIDENCE:
5 MORE MOB MOVIES YOU CAN'T REFUSE

1. *Get Carter* (1971, UK; Mike Hodges, dir.)
America wasn't the only place undergoing a revolution in mob movies; with this visceral crime drama, featuring Michael Caine exacting brutal revenge for the death of his brother, Britain got in on the act as well.

Mike Hodges' gloomy depiction of Newcastle's urban slums reflected the gritty feel of New York crime films of the same period.

2. Shaft (1971, USA; Gordon Parks, dir.)

One of the first and greatest of the blaxploitation films of the 1970s, *Shaft* featured crisp direction by the great photographer Gordon Parks, a fierce lead performance by Richard Roundtree, and a classic Isaac Hayes score. *Shaft* was fairly daring for its time, playing up the racial tensions between black criminals in Harlem and the New York Mafia.

3. Charley Varrick (1973, USA; Don Siegel, dir.)

The Mafia are the villains in this gripping little heist/revenge hybrid, but the good guy isn't a cop or a federal agent—it's aging bank robber Walter Matthau, who has accidently ripped off a mob money-laundering operation. Another enjoyable effort from Don Siegel's most fertile period.

4. Zanjeer (1973, IND; Prakash Mehra, dir.)

At the same time *The Godfather* was transforming American crime cinema, *Zanjeer*—the story of a young police inspector who has vowed revenge on the mob that slaughtered his family—was doing the same for Indian film. It made a fortune, shifted public attention from romances to action films, and made a star of Amitabh Bachchan, who played its brooding hero.

5. Bring Me the Head of Alfredo Garcia (1974, USA; Sam Peckinpah, dir.)

One of the first on-screen depictions of the Mexican mob comes in this existential action film, with the great Warren Oates as a small-time hustler looking to make easy money from a vengeful mobster. Director Sam Peckinpah is best known for his groundbreaking westerns, but this underrated film shows him to be just as effective in a contemporary setting.

And there, for all their similarities, may lie the most profound difference between *The Godfather* and *The Sopranos*. Michael Corleone lives in a Grand Guignol world, an operatic tragedy from which he cannot escape despite his own best intentions. Tony Soprano lives in the legacy of that world, where the operatic has degraded to the soap-operatic, where theatrical melodrama has curdled into the prosaic demands of the everyday. Every conflict seems smaller (if no less compelling to the viewer): Vito Corleone worried that his son would be trapped in the same cycle of bloodshed and revenge from which he emerged, while Tony Soprano worries that his son might be a dullard not suited for anything but playing video games. Michael's betrayals are grand and epic—brother turning against brother and wife against husband for profound emotional reasons. Tony's betrayals are petty and small, with friends turning on friends in exchange for a few years sheared off a prison sentence for second-rate drug charges and RICO violations. Even the murders Tony commits seem tawdry and gross compared with the larger-than-life killings in the *Godfather* movies. He, too, is a prisoner, not only of his own wicked deeds, but also of a world in which they yield rewards far less grand.

MEAN STREETS AND THE AUTEUR ERA

The rise of "maverick cinema" is so well documented at this point that movies have been made about the movies that constituted the movement. The arrival in Hollywood of young, daring directors with rebellious attitudes and backgrounds in independent cinema—and the subsequent and surprising success they had in creating movies widely embraced by the American public—is the subject of a number of excellent documentaries, books, and academic studies. The maverick moviemakers of the 1960s and 1970s were a major reason for the shift away from the studio system, the fading away of the Hays Code (and its replacement by the MPAA ratings system)—and of course, for transforming the very nature of the crime film.

The mavericks were not emerging from a vacuum, and their embrace of low-culture conceits, as embodied by the gangster film, was not without precedent. The work of directors like Robert Altman, Francis Ford Coppola, William Friedkin, Brian De Palma, and John Milius was presaged in the rise of what French critics dubbed the "auteur" movement. The director was the author of a film, responsible for its feeling, its tone, and its mood just as much as, or more than, its screenwriter. Many of the minds behind this theory emerged as directors themselves, forming the spine of the French nouvelle vague movement that took European cinema by storm in the late 1950s and early 1960s. Like the mavericks who would follow in their footsteps, they were obsessed with topics thought beneath the concerns of "serious" filmmakers: crime, urban squalor, the working class, the low-born, and junk culture.

Martin Scorsese—the filmmaker perhaps more responsible than anyone save David Chase for *The Sopranos'* existence, and the man referred to by its characters as "Marty"—was at the vanguard of the maverick film movement. He saw the idea of a director as the author of a motion picture become received wisdom. The first of Scorsese's films to receive widespread public and critical attention was 1973's *Mean Streets*, and any number of qualities that would come to characterize his later work were already present there in embryonic form. It was his first collaboration with Robert De Niro, who would star in many of his greatest films. It incorporated a seamless rock soundtrack that heightened the emotional effect of each scene. And it employed fast, precise editing to convey a sense of energy and rhythm that made other movies feel like they were stuck in amber.

Vitally to the kind of storytelling that would later characterize *The Sopranos*, *Mean Streets*—the story of a low-level mob runner who takes a proprietary interest in the safety of his self-destructive, reckless friend—depicted life in the Mafia not for sensationalistic violence or exploitation, but because Scorsese felt these criminals were interesting people with inherently compelling stories. This heady mix of psychological compulsion and damaged Catholicism would become a blueprint for Scorsese's finest work—and one of the richest veins David Chase would tap for *The Sopranos*.

THE FRENCH CONNECTION
AND THE RISE OF DRUG GANGS

Dealing drugs has always been a profitable activity for organized criminals. Even before Al Capone made millions bootlegging liquor, there was a brisk trade in opium both in the U.S. and overseas. But after the Second World War turned the world into a smaller place. The massive influx of heroin and cocaine into the States led to a moral panic over drugs the likes of which America had never seen. And, more relevantly, a vast new demand for drugs created new opportunities for organized crime, but also put pressures on them that would eventually cause many groups to splinter and fall.

The French Connection, released in 1971 and the first R-rated film to win an Academy Award for Best Picture, was a success by every possible measure. It cemented the reputations of director William Friedkin and stars Gene Hackman and Roy Scheider; it won multiple Oscars; its title instantly entered the popular vernacular; and it delivered a chase scene so stunning that second-rate copies of it became mandatory in action films for decades. But it also marked a turning point in the police procedural and was one of the first important films to deal with a major shift in both how organized crime operated and law enforcement's response to it.

Crime films had been dealing with the drug culture since they were invented. Plenty of pre-Code classics feature drug scenes, and in the '60s, when youth culture became fully entwined with drug culture, there was no shortage of movies dealing with the straight crowd's horrified reaction to the new wave of casual drug use. But *The French Connection* changed things. Not only did it feature a decidedly unromantic look at law enforcement—Hackman's Popeye Doyle, while a good cop and a relentless foe of crime, is a rather unpleasant human being on any number of levels—but it also gave audiences a new, and grim, understanding of the role drugs were beginning to play in society. It alerted viewers to the vast amounts of money to be made in the drug trade and how that money corrupted law enforcement and the justice system. It played up the international nature of drug smuggling, an activity that by the early 1970s literally reached around the world. And it let the way heroin was destroying the inner cities speak for itself.

The massive expansion and bottomless harm done by the drug trade had reached a new level of reality, one that would be reflected in every gangster movie that followed *The French Connection*. In the following year, *The Godfather* addressed the way the drug trade caused massive rifts in the way Mafia families did business. By the 1980s, the cocaine trade surpassed the heroin trade, and destructive mandatory sentencing was introduced into law to try to combat it. It was these stiff penalties that caused many a mobster to turn state's evidence to avoid a lengthy jail term—a decision we see made by a number of *Sopranos* characters, from Big Pussy to Adriana.

AL PACINO, THE UNLIKELY GODFATHER

In addition to its many other virtues and the way it transformed the modern notion of the crime drama, *The Godfather* scored a number of casting coups. It reintroduced Marlon Brando and Sterling Hayden to the public, launched the careers of Diane Keaton and Talia Shire, and provided John Cazale and Robert Castellano with their definitive screen performances. But most of all, it made a huge star out of a relatively unknown thirty-year-old actor named Al Pacino, who greatly transformed the way mob bosses were portrayed on film.

Pacino almost didn't get the role that launched him to the highest tier of Hollywood actors. Paramount notoriously hated him—they'd wanted a handsome, all-American type like Robert Redford or Ryan O'Neal for the role of the promising young war hero Michael Corleone. Director Francis Ford Coppola bristled at the idea of casting a non-Italian in the role, while the studio complained that Pacino was too short, too unattractive, and too unknown to stake so much money on. Compromises were proposed (James Caan, who would eventually play Sonny, was slotted to play Michael instead), but when Coppola threatened to walk out on filming and cause Paramount to lose millions in work already completed, the studio relented. With Pacino confirmed as Michael, a star was born—and a profound shift occurred in the movie industry's approach to casting.

With a few notable exceptions, crime bosses in the past had been archetypal tough guys, either big burly goons or small, mean-spirited heels. Even when the actors playing them delivered an excellent performance, little attention was paid to any subtleties or shadings. These were bad men because it was their nature; their character was determined by nothing more than having been born and raised to get what they wanted through force and intimidation.

The tragedy of Michael Corleone in *The Godfather*, though, was a far more delicate and complex narrative, one that had to be carried off by an actor who could provide a face and a voice to the deep psychological tragedy of a good man who has a chance to escape the evil legacy of his family, but who cannot bring himself to do so because of the love that family gave him. Slight, sensitive, with a quiet voice and a calm, centered demeanor, handsome but without a matinee idol's good looks—and most of all, able to convey precisely the heartbreaking contradiction of a man who destroys his family by trying his best to protect it Al Pacino was the perfect choice.

Though Tony Soprano was a throwback to previous generations of gangsters rather than a psychological descendent of Michael Corleone (if Michael had such an heir in the world of *The Sopranos*, Johnny Sacramoni may be the closest to it), Pacino's performance still set the tone for the show. He created the role of a reticent criminal overlord whose ingrained psychological issues dictated, and sometimes hindered, his behavior—a pattern easily seen in Vito Spatafore, Tony Blundetto, and many others.

BLACK CAESAR AND BLAXPLOITATION

The relationship between the Mafia, with its ties to old Europe and its emphasis on family bonds and ancient rituals, and America's black criminal gangs, with their access to the underclass and their sometimes desperate fearlessness, has changed significantly over the years, and this reality is reflected in mob movies. That Italian organized crime outfits harbored virulent racism against African-Americans is a matter of court records as well as Hollywood films. Evidence of it can be seen in *The Godfather*, when the Five Families vow to confine the drug trade to black communities ("They're animals anyway, so let them lose their souls") and in *The Sopranos*, when Tony and his crew simultaneously farm out their dirty work to black hoodlums and blame them for the mobsters' own failures and misdeeds.

Most ethnic criminal enterprises arise from groups that are traditionally excluded from the legitimate American power structure, and no group has been more systematically excluded than blacks. As a result, they've been involved in all sorts of nefarious activities, but long before the rise of the Crips and Bloods, there were black kingpins finding ways to turn penny-ante rackets into profitable organized crime. The numbers rackets were originally controlled by black crime bosses and were only later folded into the Mafia's portfolio through intimidation. The same pattern occurred in the drug trade: marijuana, heroin, and crack were initially the domain of black gangsters before more established crime syndicates realized the vast amount of money to be had out of it.

The notion of representation is a powerful one in popular culture. Groups who were historically not portrayed in television, cinema, and literature felt even more marginalized by their cultural invisibility, to the extent that they began to flock even to questionable depictions of themselves in the media. Better to be shown as evil, after all, than to be completely absent. Blacks bristled under police harassment, but starting in the early 1970s, the "blaxploitation" genre, with its low-budget, high-energy films featuring African-Americans in the roles of badass cops and sinister mob bosses, won huge numbers of fans in the inner cities. The black characters were often stereotypical, degraded, even offensive—but black moviegoers were still drawn to any film that showed people like them exercising genuine power.

Black Caesar, an early blaxploitation effort from 1973 directed by cut-rate auteur Larry Cohen, is one of the best examples of the genre. A more or less straight-up remake of *Little Caesar* with ex-jock Fred Williamson in the Edward G. Robinson role, it stands out because of its fierce energy, above-average performances, colorful script, and tremendous soundtrack by James Brown and his bandleader Fred Wesley. It also highlights the uncomfortable relationship between the Mafia and its black counterparts. White audiences paid it little mind, but black ones loved it, and it became a cultural touchstone for what would become an entire generation of hip-hop musicians. While Tony Soprano was blaming his troubles on "unidentified black males," they were creating a parallel criminal culture all their own.

SCARFACE
AND THE SPLINTERING OF THE "FAMILY" FILM

One of those rare films that becomes incredibly memorable and culturally influential without actually being that good, Brian De Palma's 1983 crime epic *Scarface* remade the 1932 Howard Hawks gangster flick for a new reality. Al Pacino, as lurid and over the top here as he was subtle and understated in *The Godfather*, plays sneering, animalistic Cuban refugee Tony Montana. While elements of traditional gangster drama remain, especially in his overprotective attitude toward his little sister/Madonna-whore stand-in (played by Mary Elizabeth Mastrantonio), Montana's rise to the top of Miami's drug underworld is accomplished through terrifying violence and the utter betrayal of anyone who stands in his way. Loyalty, tradition, and honor are laughed off as jokes from an ancient past, mere obstacles to the acquisition of money, power, and women.

De Palma's film was overblown, overacted, and often nonsensical. But it was also nearly perfect as an act of iconography, a movie *as* a movie: from its unforgettable poster to the grotesque acts of violence it featured (helicopter lynchings and chain saw executions among them), from its hammy but quotable lines to its palette of bright reds and stark whites, the new *Scarface* caught the imagination of a generation. At the same time that it pointed out the direction crime films would take for the next decade, it captured the attention of millions of gangsters and gangster wannabes. Its influence on popular culture was huge, especially in the world of hip-hop.

The movie's influence on *The Sopranos* is just as vast. It isn't just that the show exists in the changed world reflected in the movie, where drugs make fortunes, violence is degrading instead of efficient, and tradition always takes a backseat to power. It's that the characters live in a world where *Scarface* exists, and it is as big a part of their psyches as are the *Godfather* movies. The Soprano crew are as media-savvy as they are criminally efficient—probably more so. Nowhere is this more pronounced than in "Meadowlands," when Christopher Moltisanti, urging a strong response to a power play by Uncle Junior's men, says, "This ain't negotiation time. This is *Scarface*, final scene, fuckin' bazookas under each arm, 'Say hello to my little friend!'" (Silvio Dante, himself an inveterate quoter of *The Godfather*, responds: "Always with the scenarios.")

Scarface accomplished for its time what *Psycho* did for its own. Where *Psycho* silently cut the throat of the traditional era of crime dramas, ushering in an age of psychopaths and maniacs, *Scarface* noisily exploded the era of traditional mob movies, slaughtering the staid traditions of Mafia families and dragging the entire concept of the mob movie kicking and screaming into the bloody, cocaine-fueled action era of the 1980s. And like the revolution *Psycho* started twenty years earlier, the transformation wasn't entirely for the best: the following decade saw sophisticated crime drama take a nosedive, largely replaced in the public consciousness by gory, noisy, enervating action movies with an endless succession of colorless renegade cops and militaristic vigilantes. It was a change that seemed inevitable, though, and De Palma ushered it in with style and vision.

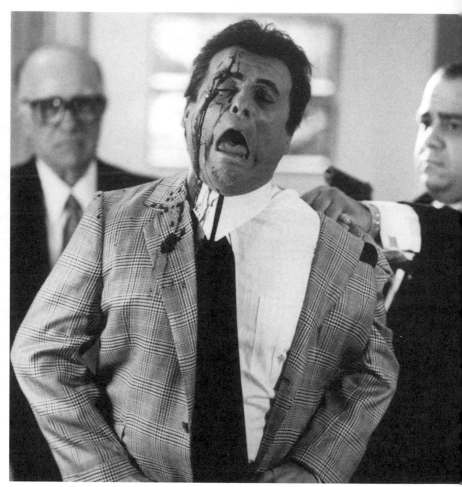

Joe Pesci in *GoodFellas*. (Warner Bros. Pictures/Photofest)

5

THIS IS THE BAD TIME:
THE MOB IN DECLINE

GOODFELLAS

If one were looking for the blueprint of *The Sopranos*—for the text it drew on most heavily to build its tone, its structure, its themes, and its entire approach to telling a story about both crime and human drama—one would have a fiercely difficult time deciding between *The Godfather* and *GoodFellas*. As noted in the previous chapter, *The Godfather* and its first sequel, which gave the culture its archetypal Mafia epic, were probably the greatest influence on the *characters* of *The Sopranos*; the people who inhabit David Chase's fictional world watch Francis Ford Coppola's movies, quote them, and even do their best to live them. But when it comes to the *show*, there is probably nothing more influential than *GoodFellas*, Chase's self-identified Bible, a vision of the Mafia epic gone sour.

The essential differences between *The Godfather* and *GoodFellas* are the very building blocks of *The Sopranos*. The story of Tony Soprano and his family and crew takes place in a world that is the aesthetic, economic, stylistic, and philosophical heir to the latter (just as *GoodFellas* itself is to the former). While Coppola's film exuded an epic quality that placed it in the tradition of the greatest products of the Golden Age of Hollywood, Scorsese was a master of creating the same addictive character arcs while framing them on a smaller and more realistic scale. *The Godfather* represents for Tony Soprano the ideal of what he strives for, the illusion of grandeur that he chases and can never achieve. This is made explicit when one of A.J.'s high school friends asks why his family doesn't have "Corleone money." And it is in *GoodFellas* that the decay of the dream is first made explicit on screen: even during the good times, for Henry Hill and his crew, there is a sense of downsizing, of scaling back, of giving up one corrupt dream for another—a lesser dream, no less violent but with a far higher ratio of blood to money. Like Jimmy Conway's crew, the Soprano gang exists, on a parallel plane to the New York families, and a somewhat lesser one. For both groups, accidents of birth and different approaches to tradition bar them from entry to the centuries-old mores of the Sicilians. When Phil Leotardo complains that the DiMeo family will "make anyone" and doesn't abide by the proper Mafia traditions, he is reacting to them the way the Corleones would react to Joe Pesci's Tommy DeVito. *GoodFellas* is placed at exactly the center of the fulcrum: the promise of *The Godfather* is broken and scattered, and *The Sopranos* are living in the new reality *GoodFellas* represents.

It is not necessary to even look beyond the surface to see how profoundly *GoodFellas* influenced David Chase. It is from Scorsese, and most clearly from *GoodFellas*, that *The Sopranos* took its use of musical cues and integration of the soundtrack with the action on screen. Both stories take place in a time when the greatest threat to the mob came not from without, but from within, with the threat of heavy drug sentencing causing many wiseguys to turn state's evidence. Much like Ray Liotta's Henry Hill, the mobsters of the DiMeo family are often themselves addicted to drugs, tied down to family obligations that hinder their criminal activities, or trapped in marriages where neither partner is getting what he or she wants. Certainly Chase was not shy about borrowing cast members from his Bible: Lorraine Bracco, Tony Darrow, Frank Vincent, Michael Imperioli, and Tony Lip all appear in both the movie and the series. Even Tony's first murder—of a black bookie named Willie Overall—is reminiscent of *GoodFellas'* portrayal of the killing of "Stacks" Edwards.

Above and beyond such cast pilfering, though, *The Sopranos* is seeded with ideas, characters, and techniques from *GoodFellas*. Tommy DeVito is the archetype of the troublesome, violent brute, too impatient and hotheaded to play by the rules, who would later turn up in characters like Richie Aprile and Ralph Cifaretto. Henry Hill's contempt for squares and average joes, the derisive laughter he directs at his wife's parents and others not in on the game, presages Tony's inability to relate to the *medigans* who are part of normal society. Despite being set in an earlier time, *GoodFellas* could be considered the first of the postfeminist mob films, and in Karen Hill we see an early echo of Carmela Soprano, the independent-minded woman simultaneously attracted to and repelled by criminal violence (and its material rewards). And again, the masterful use of music to set the tone and mood was pioneered by Scorsese and perfected by Chase and his team.

But describing it this way makes it seem like *The Sopranos* is nothing but a rip-off of *GoodFellas*, and nothing could be further from the truth. If it were just a rip-off, that would be understandable, even forgivable: *GoodFellas* is a masterwork with scenes so iconic that it is almost impossible to avoid its influence. Like *The Godfather*, it has been endlessly riffed on and parodied, and some of its most famous scenes have become part of our shared cultural language. But *The Sopranos* is more than just an imitator. It is an inheritor, a work of art that takes its influences and develops them, moves them forward in new directions. While Martin Scorsese didn't invent the montage, his mastery of it allowed him to take small-scale storytelling and give it an epic quality; his ability to compress events into intelligently cut scenes is what allows him to transform volumes of narrative material into short, unforgettable scenes. What Chase pulls off, in a rather spectacular reversal, is to unpack all the material that Scorsese compresses. He shows in full detail what his predecessor leaves out, eschewing the traditional wisdom that it is always better to show less—and the miracle is that it works. ☞

SUPPORTING EVIDENCE:
5 MORE MASTERPIECES OF THE MOB IN DECLINE

1. *Chinatown* (1974, USA; Roman Polanski, dir.)
At a time when it appeared the mob movie might take over the world,

Roman Polanski and writer Robert Towne saw an aesthetic dead end and moved forward by looking back. A brilliant return to and reinvention of film noir, the story takes place in 1937 Los Angeles, but reeks of the decay of Hollywood forty years later.

2. *Dog Day Afternoon* (1975, USA; Sidney Lumet, dir.)

Fresh off of *The Godfather* films, Al Pacino and John Cazale are electrifying as a pair of would-be bank robbers who engineer—and then botch—a job to finance a sex-change operation for Pacino's wife. Its rebellious tone, sympathy with the hapless criminals, and insightful look at the lightning-quick way public opinion can shift for or against people have made it a classic.

3. *The Killing of a Chinese Bookie* (1976, USA; John Cassavetes, dir.)

John Cassavetes, the patron saint of American independent cinema, had dabbled in crime films before; his *Gloria* is considered to be one of the all-time great depictions of a gangster's moll. But this film is the Mafia movie at its lowest ebb: the "hero" is a tawdry strip club owner with a gambling addiction, the mobsters are as low-rent as they are physically grotesque, and the whole film is infused with a sleaziness that couldn't be further from the gold-paneled world of *The Godfather*.

4. *The Long Good Friday* (1980, UK; John Mackenzie, dir.)

This brilliant look at the decay, not only of the old-time British crime syndicates, but an entire British way of life, is a triumph. Bob Hoskins stars as a mobster looking to consolidate his power with the American Mafia and make millions in legitimate business, only to see his world come apart at the hands of an unknown enemy.

5. *Sonatine* (1993, JAP; Takeshi Kitano, dir.)

A world-weary yakuza boss finds himself set up by a rival and flees to a beach house to gather his thoughts before spearheading a violent reprisal. That simple plot belies the exquisite tension that director/star Takeshi "Beat" Kitano cranks up in this galvanizing crime film. Seijun Suzuki put the yakuza film on the map, but Kitano reinvented it.

Where *GoodFellas* only hints at the banality and awkwardness of mob life, *The Sopranos* makes it the key to the entire story. Karen

Hill hides guns and money around her house, and brushes on the "harassment" her family suffers at the hands of federal agents; for Carmela Soprano, these activities are part of her entire character arc. David Chase pays tribute to Tommy DeVito's shooting of Spider by casting Michael Imperioli in a key role and having him perpetrate a similarly hotheaded act in the first season of *The Sopranos*—but more than that, he shows us what Spider's life must be like, and how people like Henry Hill and Jimmy Conway had to deal with it. With more storytelling space and time, *The Sopranos* can tell us about not only the major characters, but the minor ones as well, and the trouble they can cause for the men at the top. Chase uses the luxury of time granted by a television series to give great, rich psychological depth to characters whose *GoodFellas* forebears are mere hints and suggestions. The women with whom Henry Hill carries on his affairs have hardly any dialogue, barely any personalities; they are simply shorthand for the lusts that drive him. In *The Sopranos*, Tony's *comàres* still manage to reflect his appetites and his personality disorders, but they are also characters of real depth, with their own desires, motivations, and flaws. Scorsese and co-writer Nicholas Pileggi engage in some clever structural foreshadowing, as when Henry assures his wife that only "nigger stickup men" go to jail, because they "fall asleep in the getaway car"—anticipating the later scene where his black co-conspirator, "Stacks" Edwards, goes on the nod with the transport truck from the Lufthansa heist parked outside his apartment. But Chase trumps this narrative trick, raising it to an entirely new level by using Tony's dreams—beautifully realized on screen, full of hidden clues, and charged with a sanguinary mysticism eschewed by the street realist Scorsese—to foretell future events and illuminate new developments.

There are also fascinating parallels in the anxious and paranoid tone of both *GoodFellas* and *The Sopranos*. Though Chase's series made psychological revelations front and center—in fact, built its entire premise around them—the differences between it and Scorsese's film are far more in approach than in kind. Allowed the luxury of six years in which to plumb the depths of Tony Soprano's psyche and to see how its obsessions and obstructions poison every aspect of the mobster's home and professional life, Chase was able to take his time and reveal aspects of Tony's past in increments. He relied on the strengths of writers like Terence Winter and Michael Imperioli to reveal, through plot and character, the disintegration of Tony's mental state and the way the people around him enable it. In contrast, locked into the confines of a mainstream movie's run time, Scorsese used fantastic directing and editing to show Henry Hill's descent into drug-fueled paranoia and despair. He worked with cinematographer Michael Ballhaus and editor Thelma Schoonmaker to visually deliver the same effect—in spectacular scenes like Ray Liotta and Lorraine Bracco's elated stroll through the back rooms of the Copacabana, and Liotta's unnerving final meeting with De Niro—that Chase would later unfold textually in *The Sopranos*.

Of particular interest are the ways in which the two filmmakers approached reality—and broke with it—to deliver important tonal shifts. Scorsese is no fantasist; his films are rooted in a gritty, dirty reality, even when presented (as in *Gangs of New York*) in a highly mythologized fashion. His most absurd moments, especially *After Hours* and *The King of Comedy*, still manage to present themselves in an outsize but more or less naturalistic way. He would not allow himself, in a film as tightly controlled as *GoodFellas*, the indulgence of anything like a dream sequence; even the helicopter following Henry Hill turns out to be real and not a coke-fueled hallucination. The movie's sole break from the constraints of traditional narrative comes at the very end, when Henry Hill, betraying his oldest partners to a packed courtroom to save his own skin, steps off the witness stand to lament being cast out of the Eden that is organized crime. It is a shocking moment, but one that hammers home an essential aspect of Hill's psyche: he is a selfish egotist who, as he turns rat on the killers he willingly served, accepts no blame or responsibility, feels no guilt or shame, and can only beg the viewer to feel sorry for him and his loss of status. David Chase conversely and contradictorily shows both more ambition and more control: the dream sequences of Tony, Paulie, Carmela, and others are far more indulgent and fantastic than anything we would ever expect from Scorsese. And yet they allow Chase a freedom of expression, a means of furthering the narrative, and a vehicle for psychological insight that isn't in Scorsese's toolbox. Even in the most ambitious of Tony's dreams and visions, it is unthinkable that Tony Soprano would ever directly address the camera. But those dreams are no less jarring, no less a break from the "reality" on screen, and no less revealing of the main character's fractured psyche than are the final moments of *GoodFellas*.

None of these developments should be thought to imply that *GoodFellas* is a flawed film; it is nearly perfect. Scorsese made exactly the film he wanted, and the evidence of his success is right there for anyone to see. *The Sopranos* doesn't correct any mistakes. David Chase took advantage of the opportunities offered to him by his medium, and did new and intriguing things with the crime drama, just as Coppola and Scorsese had done before him. He built upward and outward from what Scorsese had given him with *GoodFellas*, just as Scorsese had done with Coppola's *Godfather* and Coppola had done with the filmmakers who preceded him. There are through-lines everywhere you look: the devastating cost of organized crime to a family structures; spectacular, operatic, almost Grand Guignol–style murders; and the increasingly disproportionately high cost of blood assigned to every ill-gotten dollar. But these thematic similarities shouldn't blind viewers to the essence of each. David Chase took a perfectly designed building, and constructed an entire city around it. If *GoodFellas* is the Bible, *The Sopranos* is the religion.

ATLANTIC CITY AND THE DEATH OF THE OLD WAYS

One of the most lasting themes in mob films—and certainly one that resonates in *The Sopranos* from the first episode to the blackout at the end of "Made in America"—is the decline of the old way of life. Its decay and degradation haunt Tony Soprano; no matter his material wealth and success, he feels that he no longer has access to a world of true greatness. That it may never have existed matters not even a little—in his spirit-plagued world, Tony will live forever under the shadow of his father, Johnny-Boy, who in Tony's memory is not a second-rate thug who smoked himself to death, but the symbol of a golden era of Mafia glory.

GoodFellas may be the most elegant expression of the notion that the mob suffered a precipitate fall from its "glorious time," but it wasn't the first. Mobsters were likely complaining about the long-gone world of the good old days the minute Prohibition was repealed, but one of the first and finest cinematic statements of this phenomenon was Louis Malle's *Atlantic City*, released in 1980, a full decade before Martin Scorsese gave us his object lesson on the decline of organized crime. Malle was more than familiar with crime dramas, but with *Atlantic City*, he delivers a film that is entirely different than most of the movies in this book. It's a quiet, contemplative, sweet, almost romantic movie—but one that's no less effective for those qualities.

Burt Lancaster, projecting a carefully cultivated dignity, plays Lou, a former mob functionary who claims to have been a big shot in the Las Vegas Mafia, but who is now reduced to running minor errands for his neighbor, a widowed fading star with fading looks. Into Lou's quiet life in Atlantic City comes Sally (Susan Sarandon), a waitress hoping to cash in on the city's gambling scene. She also brings with her an ex-husband mixed up in the drug trade and a pile of money that all parties involved see as their way out of a world that is crumbling around them. Unfortunately for everyone, the owners of the drugs aren't ready to give them up so easily, and when Lou steps into the role of big shot and protector, he finds it isn't as chivalric and idyllic as he'd imagined.

Malle (in conjunction with playwright John Guare, who wrote the screenplay for *Atlantic City*) avoids almost all the clichés of a gangster film, infusing *Atlantic City* with a beautiful, elegiac tone. But he doesn't sidestep the vital lessons we take away from the film and into the future of *The Sopranos*: Lancaster's longing for the vanished beauty of the old Atlantic City, where even the ocean looked better, may be sincere, but his own self-perception as an exiled king, a high roller fallen on low times, is a delusion. It's one that costs him dearly when he is force to confront the new and deadly realities of a generation of mobsters who hold no truck with sentiment.

BIG DEAL ON MADONNA STREET AND MOB COMEDIES

A sure sign that any genre of fiction is heading for the autumn of its years is the willingness to turn it into farce. Once a breed of story is open for comedy—whether satire, parody, or pure clowning—all bets are off. There were mob movies with comedic elements before the appearance of *Big Deal on Madonna Street*, but never had pure comedy been draped so gracefully over the framework of a crime drama, to such wonderful effect. It opened up an entirely new approach and set a standard for the crime comedy so high that it's rarely been approached, let alone surpassed.

Made in 1958 and inspired by the wave of French heist pictures that preceded it (*Rififi* is a particularly obvious touchstone), *Big Deal on Madonna Street* presents itself in tone and mood as a fairly straightforward crime film, with little to tip the hilarious character development that would drive it off the rails. Director Mario Monicelli presents the story of a handful of would-be thieves looking to make an easy killing off of what they believe to be an unprotected safe above an uninhabited apartment; forsaking the obvious chances for buffoonery, he sticks to a largely realist approach in his direction, and lets the humor unfold from the slow unfolding of everyone's utter unsuitability to the task. (Which isn't to say he doesn't engage in some dead-on jokes when the mood suits him. One killer moment involves Carlo Pisacane searching for a potential accomplice named Mario; a street kid informs him there are a thousand men in the neighborhood by that name. Pisacane replies that the one he's looking for is a notorious thief, only to be told that doesn't narrow the field at all.)

Monicelli forgoes immediate comic payoff in favor of a slow, hilarious build as he establishes that no one involved with the enterprise, from luckless lug Vittorio Gassman to unmotivated collaborator Totò, really has any idea how to go about it. When it came time to give a comic twist to the heist film, America's contribution was the caper, but it let its humor arise from situation—the criminals involved were still usually allowed to be skilled professionals. The genius of *Big Deal on Madonna Street* was to make them incompetents—not idiots, just people who allowed themselves, as so many real-world criminals do, to get in over their heads for a big payoff.

Combining comedy and crime would become more and more commonplace as the years went by, but most such films went for easy parody or wide comic farce. The true heirs of Monicelli's masterpiece are more likely the films of Joel and Ethan Coen, especially *Fargo*, *Burn After Reading*, *The Big Lebowski*, and even the earlier and broader *Raising Arizona*. The Coens tended to be a bit more dark, but they drew on his notion of a slow burn, a situation born of incompetence spiraling out of control and driven by a handful of people who overestimate their own menace.

ROBERT DE NIRO, THE FACE OF MODERN CRIME

There is no evidence whatsoever that Robert De Niro, the bohemian son of a pair of well-regarded painters, has anything whatsoever to do with real-world organized crime. A respected figure in his community, a generous humanitarian, and one of the most celebrated actors in motion picture history, De Niro is a beloved member of the entertainment industry, and not at all a murderous criminal who has overseen any number of nefarious enterprises. And yet it's almost impossible to look at him and *not* see a sinister figure who would just as soon put a bullet in your brain as shake your hand. He's just that good.

De Niro began working with Martin Scorsese at age twenty, and it is through Scorsese that he's become an iconic figure. Scorsese cast him in such unforgettable criminal roles as the fiery Johnny Boy in *Mean Streets*, the alienated Travis Bickle in *Taxi Driver*, the furious Jake LaMotta in *Raging Bull*, the desperate Rupert Pupkin in *The King of Comedy*, the calculating Jimmy Conway in *GoodFellas*, the psychotic Max Cady in *Cape Fear*, and the brilliant Ace Rothstein in *Casino*. And though he's an extremely diverse and versatile actor who has played any number of characters from all walks of life, even other directors have recognized De Niro's particular genius at portraying members of the criminal underworld. Francis Ford Coppola cast him as the young Vito Corleone in *The Godfather Part II*. Sergio Leone, in his excursion into the gangster flick, made him

"Noodles" Aaronson in *Once Upon a Time in America*. Michael Mann made him professional criminal Neil McCauley in *Heat*. Hell, Alan Parker even made him Satan in *Angel Heart*. There's something in the man, as with all the great mob boss actors, that exudes menace.

That's part of the reason he is so beloved of, and such an influence on, the characters of *The Sopranos*. The man they call "Bobby D." is even more an icon to them than he is to the rest of the country; because of his perceived role as a player—and despite his complete removal from the world of organized crime—he is exempted from their normal contempt for people involved in soft occupations such as the arts. It is his status as a vibrant backer of the New York film community that legitimizes Christopher's dabbling in that world; it is his status as a prominent restaurateur that enables the Sopranos' pretense as Italian gourmets. It can fairly be said of the DiMeo crew that where De Niro is concerned, they have trouble telling fantasy from reality.

There is a great temptation for actors to let their roles overtake them. One of the unfortunate characteristics of some of the *Sopranos* actors is that they have crossed the line between the world of cinematic crime and the far more dangerous world of actual illegal activity. It is a line that De Niro, as immersed in his roles as he's become, has never crossed—a testament to both his skill and his character.

A BETTER TOMORROW AND ASIAN MOBSTERS

Asian cinema had been producing crime dramas for decades when Hong Kong filmmaker John Woo debuted his film *A Better Tomorrow* in 1986. Aside from a few rarities treasured by cineastes, however, such as Akira Kurosawa's noir-style crime films and Seijun Suzuki's ultra-stylish yakuza pictures, few Asian gangster movies had any kind of impact in the West. *A Better Tomorrow* changed all that. It set off a tidal wave of imitators, introduced an entirely new genre of action filmmaking with its own tropes and cinematic language, and brought a new wave of Hong Kong filmmakers to international prominence, invigorating a regional cinema previously known only for kung fu movies.

Woo, who got his start making those martial arts films, had been in the Hong Kong movie business for more than a decade and was undergoing a significant professional slump. His colleague Tsui Hark persuaded him to keep at it and produced the film that would go on to make millions and set off a revolution in Asian cinema. One of the first films to feature the high-impact, slow-motion, gymnastic action known as "gun fu," with close-quarters firearm battles taking the place of punches and kicks, *A Better Tomorrow* also pioneered the style of cinema known as "heroic bloodshed," so called for its balletic violence and its almost medieval morality plays. The genre often featured incorruptible cops, criminals with extremely rigorous codes of honor, intense (almost homoerotic) male bonding, and devastating displays of gun violence involving the Chinese organized crime syndicates known as triads.

A Better Tomorrow tells the story of two triad mobsters—Sung Tse-Ho (Ti Lung) and Mark Lee (Asian cinema icon Chow Yun-Fat)—who are the best of friends but find themselves forced to deal with both a ruthless new recruit named Shing and Ho's young brother Kit, who wants to become a policeman. The story, influenced by the kinetic work of Martin Scorsese as much as it is the athletic heroism of traditional *wuxia* films, involves betrayal, honor, and a fatalistic sense of inevitable tragedy that is the only means of redemption for these blood-soaked characters. It struck such a chord with viewers at home and abroad that it became a cultural phenomenon, inspiring two sequels and endless rip-offs. Its visual style became the norm for Hong Kong action and eventually made its way to America, influencing movies as far-ranging as *The Matrix*. Even the costumes caused a sensation: Chow Yun-Fat's trench coats and Alain Delon–style sunglasses were worn by tens of thousands of trendy imitators. The heroic bloodshed genre would produce a number of classics, including Ringo Lam's *City On Fire* (from which Quentin Tarantino borrowed liberally for *Reservoir Dogs*) and Woo's own *The Killer* and *Hard Boiled*. Its impact in China was almost inestimable, comparable to that of *The Godfather* in America—and more important, it put a new and lively kind of gangster movie on the map. Woo's success record in Hollywood is a mixed bag, but he launched a revolution whose gunshots still ring out today.

MENACE II SOCIETY
AND HOW GANGSTERS BECAME GANGSTAS

By the 1980s, the game was up for big-time African-American organized crime. Blacks had always been disproportionately targeted for drug crimes, and harsh new sentencing guidelines meant that the heroin kingpins of the '60s and '70s would be sent away for good. Crack, a devastating new form of cheap and highly addictive cocaine, would ravage the inner cities and create generations of desperate addicts. A moral panic over cocaine would lead to even more strict punishments for drug dealing. And the attempts by high-profile gangsters to organize and control their criminal enterprises would fall apart, leaving the drug trade in the hands of dozens of brutal street gangs who would rack up body counts on the level of a full-scale war.

In the late 1980s and early 1990s, these conflicts, which would turn South Central Los Angeles into a free-fire zone so lethal that even the police were reluctant to visit it, would generate a wave of crime dramas, heavily influenced by both the great gangster epics of the past and the new wave of G-funk rappers, who spun violent but celebrated stories about the hard life and the crack trade. Films like *New Jack City*, *Juice*, *Colors*, *Belly*, *Deep Cover*, *Boyz N the Hood* and *South Central* all portrayed a new urban reality previously unheard of in crime films, infinitely more nihilistic, hopeless, and despairing than what had come before.

One of the best and most influential of this wave of "hood films" was 1993's *Menace II Society*. The directorial debut of African-American siblings Allen and Albert Hughes, who would go on to become a significant Hollywood presence, the film became a touchstone of hip-hop culture and helped launch the career of Larenz Tate, who is unforgettable in the role of the rage-filled O-Dog. *Menace II Society* walks an extremely fine line, showing the wide range of factors that lead young black males to a life of crime and violence, but never completely excusing any of its protagonists for the choices they make. O-Dog and Caine, the two young men who are the film's primary focus, are faced with endless pressures: boiling inner-city racial tensions, absent or incarcerated fathers, poverty, substance abuse, police brutality, and a criminal underworld that can lead to quick money or an early death. The Hughes brothers manage to convey all these in a grimly unsensational manner, creating an oppressive mood that is hard to shake off.

The influence of hood films such as *Menace II Society* continued to resonate well into the 2000s, culminating in the HBO miniseries *The Wire*, an incredibly ambitious attempt to tie together all the social problems the Hughes brothers nodded to. The world of *The Sopranos* is intimately connected with the brutal inner-city drug trade: when Tony laments that some parts of New Jersey have become impassable thanks to the vicious, easy violence of the street gangs, he evinces a typical denial of the role he played in that ruination by extorting legitimate businesses and profiting off of the sale of drugs.

James Gandolfini and Delroy Lindo in *Get Shorty*. (MGM/Photofest)

6

THIS AIN'T NO ANCIENT CULTURE: THE PERFECT STORM OF *THE SOPRANOS*

GHOST DOG: THE WAY OF THE SAMURAI

In the 1990s, spurred by the success of *GoodFellas* **and the** emergence of a new generation of crime movie auteurs, a number of films appeared that brought the genre to the edge of the century. Several of them, whose plots, themes, and ideas are astonishingly similar to those of *The Sopranos*, were released in 1999: *Get Shorty*, with its media-savvy mobster; *The Limey*, whose protagonist is kept off the straight and narrow by a desire to protect his family; *Analyze This*, with its central conceit of a panic-prone gangster consulting a therapist; and Spike Lee's gritty, underrated *Summer of Sam*, written by Michael Imperioli. All were released the same year as *The Sopranos* made its HBO debut, arguing for a sort of artistic critical mass that would transform the crime drama and provide new approaches and new concerns to carry it into a new millennium. (Sensing this fundamental shift, many critics sat up and took notice, reckoning something was in the wind even if they couldn't figure out the pattern yet. *Entertainment Weekly* called 1999 "the year that changed movies," and obviously, a similar argument can be made for television.) But for all their surface similarities, none of these movies so closely mirrored *The Sopranos* as another release from that year by a director whose sensibilities could not be further from those of David Chase.

Ghost Dog: The Way of the Samurai was written and directed by Jim Jarmusch. No TV veteran, Jarmusch was a product of the trendy New York art scene and a critical favorite for his quirky, slow-paced comedies, which lovingly observed the losers, castoffs, and square pegs of the world. A champion of independent film, he gained attention with movies like *Stranger Than Paradise*, *Down by Law* and *Mystery Train*, and in 1995, he first tried his hand at a genre film with the spooky, elegiac western *Dead Man*. An eerie, beautiful film with a haunting Neil Young soundtrack (like David Chase, Jarmusch deserves to be mentioned alongside the likes of Quentin Tarantino and Martin Scorsese for his exceptional skill at integrating music into his films), *Dead Man* spurred him to try his hand at a gangster picture. Knowing Jarmusch, few expected it to be anything like a traditional Mafia movie—but even fewer predicted how provocative and memorable it would be. No one imagined how precisely it would anticipate *The Sopranos*.

As is the case with most of Jarmusch's films, the plot of *Ghost Dog: The Way of the Samurai* is simple: a midlevel mobster saves a young black man from an assault. Swearing fealty to him, the young man grows up to be a deadly assassin, working only for his "master" and performing every hit with invisible lethality. But when one hit goes wrong, the higher-ups order the killer killed—and the assassin visits bloody murder on his betrayers, before a final confrontation with his boss. It's a story utterly familiar to any crime movie fan, but as with Jarmusch's best work, the devil is in the details. He takes a well-worn, even predictable plot and decorates it with so many bizarre details, brilliant characterizations, knowing observations, and moments of humor and tragedy that it ends up feeling like something completely new.

Just as Tony Soprano frequently laments his living in the modern day, detached from the insubstantial golden past he conflates with the old days of the Mafia, Ghost Dog—played with a compelling, weighty sadness by the excellent Forest Whitaker, the character is never given another name—lives in a distinctly modern world, but approaches it through an ancient tradition. He uses a high-tech gadget to steal cars, listens to cutting-edge hip-hop, and wields deadly modern weapons, but his Bible is the *Hagakure*, a collection of sayings from the eighteenth-century samurai Yamamoto Tsunetomo. Ghost Dog insists on being paid only once a year, at the beginning of fall, and communicates with his boss through carrier pigeons he raises himself. Like the mobsters for whom he kills, Ghost Dog lives by an archaic code of behavior that both insulates and protects him and keeps him isolated from the world. He finds interacting with the outside world jarring; he lives alone and friendless in a rooftop perch and looks at the modern world as corrupted. (When he encounters a group of hunters who have slaughtered a bear, he lectures them about how animals were treated with more respect in days gone by, only to be told by one of the hunters that "This ain't no ancient culture here, mister." Ghost Dog replies to the contrary and murders the men.) Even his murders are carried out in a ritualistic way. Fatalistic, determined, formidable, and sensitive, Whitaker imbues the character with both great power and great emptiness; he meditates on the inevitability of death while barely seeming to be alive, his soft bulk belying his lethality and his inflexible moral code blinding him to his own unique nature. Ghost Dog is a new wrinkle on a familiar crime drama archetype: the man who is both sustained by and doomed by his code.

But he is not only a man lost in time; he is a man between cultures. The coming of the multicultural world, and the comedy and tragedy that can result from new cultures coming into close contact with old ones, is the most persistent theme in Jarmusch's work, and it shows up here in spades. Ghost Dog is an urban African-American who patterns his life on a largely rural Japanese warrior culture three centuries gone. With nothing in common with most of his peers, he chats only with a young Jamaican girl from the neighborhood whom he encourages to read the *Hagakure* and his "best friend," Raymond, a Haitian who runs an ice cream truck. In one of the film's funniest conceits, the two carry on "conversations" despite the fact that Ghost Dog speaks no French and Raymond (a lovely performance by Isaach De Bankolé) speaks no English. One of their neighbors—who in a typically Jarmuschian bit is building a boat on top of his building—speaks only Spanish, which doesn't prevent him from engaging in conversation with the other two. Further throwing things for a multicultural loop is the fact that Ghost Dog owes his allegiance to the Mafia, who don't at all share or even understand his samurai code or his peculiar rituals. It is one of the film's foremost ironies that the person with whom he has the most in common is the daughter of mob head Ray Vargo, a beautiful but emotionally deadened woman who may have lost her mind from seeing so much bloodshed.

David Chase has shown us mobsters who farm out their work to black gangbangers, and he has shown us the rift between the old-school suit-and-tie mobsters and their tracksuited young counterparts. But he never goes as far as *Ghost Dog: The Way of the Samurai*, in which Jarmusch brings us a Mafia that is not only in decline, but that doesn't even seem to recognize it. (The exception is Ghost Dog's boss, Louie, who is quite aware that the world is changing beneath his feet. He is held in low regard by the other mobsters, though, and Ghost Dog himself is blindly loyal to him, so Louie's sense that everything is different goes unheeded.) The leader of the family is Vargo, played by a sepulchral Henry Silva; as its elder statesman (aside from one out-of-it mobster who is a few exits past senile, looking for all the world like a zombie Uncle Junior) and the voice of the old ways, he is the only one who respects Ghost Dog's "poetry of war." Of course, he also looks like a walking corpse. Vargo presides over a crew—it is implied but never openly stated that like the Sopranos, they're based in New Jersey—that represents the mob in a state of decay that would give Tony a heart attack. Perpetually short of cash, they meet in the back room of a run-down Chinese restaurant that makes Satriale's Pork Store look like the Four Seasons. One of the crew clownishly recites rap lyrics, and when they send men out to hunt down Ghost Dog, it's a sly commentary on the graying of the Mafia: the hit squad consists of morbidly obese middle-aged men in cheap tracksuits who get winded halfway up a flight of stairs. They end up killing the wrong man just so they can go home and take it easy.

In contrast to the powerful but inept gangsters, Ghost Dog himself is supremely competent and, when the final showdown comes between him and his bosses, nearly unstoppable. Jarmusch brilliantly illustrates the way both sides are ultimately straitjacketed by their codes: Ghost Dog's adherence to the way of the samurai makes him a force to be reckoned with, but has also left him fatalistic, cold, and unable to deal with ordinary people. The Mafiosi's own code of honor makes them inflexible and blind, allowing them to take advantage of Ghost Dog's talents but leading them to severely underestimate him. The showdown between their respective codes gets the plot rolling, when Ghost Dog executes a mobster who fell out of favor but leaves a witness alive; it culminates at the film's end, when his boss is forced to choose between loyalty to his family and loyalty to his most faithful retainer. As is made clear—here no less than in *The Sopranos*—neither decision will lead to a good outcome.

Jim Jarmusch's films are anything but energetic, and he eschews the complex plots and sprawling casts of *The Sopranos*. His movies are often set on a slow boil, developing at a pace that allows them all the time they need, and *Ghost Dog: The Way of the Samurai* is no exception. It builds with a leisurely pace to its bloody end, and many scenes are carried with no dialogue or action, relying on the silent, mournful expressions on Whitaker's face and the stunning score by the Wu-Tang Clan's RZA to keep the viewer interested. But Jarmusch is also extraordinarily effective at delivering on the themes he has built from the outset. The film may take awhile to get going, and they may not be immediately evident, but there are small rewards in almost every frame. *Ghost Dog* isn't just about multiculturalism; as a movie, it's practically an encyclopedia of international film. Jean-Pierre Melville's *Le Samouraï* is its clearest touchstone, but it also draws on Akira Kurosawa's *Rashomon* and its themes of distorted memory, Seijun Suzuki's *Branded to Kill* and its theatrical murders, the samurai epics of Japan, and the "heroic bloodshed" films of Hong Kong. He even manages to slip in a reference to his own *Dead Man*.

But for all its references, for all the ways in which it takes viewers on a tour through other cultures, other stories, other films, *Ghost Dog: The Way of the Samurai* is no mere amalgam. It manages the rare alchemy of turning the familiar into the strange, using conventional situations to reveal something deep and new. Just as *The Sopranos* took standard mob tropes and used them to cast light on profound issues of psychology, family, and society, *Ghost Dog* draws from its multicultural stew a number of keen observations about race, tradition, and friendship. It steadfastly resists becoming a run-of-the-mill gangster action film; glimpses of lesser movies peek out here and there, but are never allowed to take over *Ghost Dog*'s thoughtful, meditative pace. When it finally gets to where it's going, it proves well worth the journey; in two hours, it manages to touch on many of the themes *The Sopranos* would explore over six years. Both stories have a great deal to say about changing urban environments, the self-defeating nature of crime and the self-deceiving moral codes of criminals, the inapplicability of old ideals to modern situations, the value and the difficulty of communication among different groups, and even the way animals represent hope to those who no longer have any in their fellow humans. Though the final products couldn't be more different, *Ghost Dog* and *The Sopranos* follow widely variant paths to arrive at almost exactly the same location. ☞

SUPPORTING EVIDENCE: 5 MORE WORTHWHILE CONTEMPORARIES OF *THE SOPRANOS*

1. *The Krays* (1990, UK; Peter Medak, dir.)

Although it appeared almost a decade before *The Sopranos*, this stylish retelling of the lives of two notorious London gangsters predicted the show's artful approach to crime drama and its twisted family dynamics. Peter Medak's direction is lovely, and Gary and Martin Kemp—best known to Americans as the '80s pop duo Spandau Ballet—are hypnotic as the Kray brothers.

2. *The Usual Suspects* (1995, USA; Bryan Singer, dir.)

In the post-Tarantino era, heist films weren't enough—they had to have a twist to make them memorable, and *The Usual Suspects* served up a doozy. Bryan Singer's slick direction put him on the map, and Christopher McQuarrie's clever script made Keyser Söze a household name.

3. *L.A. Confidential* (1997, USA; Curtis Hanson, dir.)

Novelist James Ellroy's brutally minimalist prose filters the noir shadings of the past with an even more cynical modern sensibility. Curtis Hanson's adaptation of Ellroy's novel is problematic, but it's worth seeing for its retro feel and the way it intertwines stories of gangsterism, police corruption, and celebrity obsession.

4. Dead or Alive (1999, JAP; Takashi Miike, dir.)

Building on the flashy yakuza films of Seijun Suzuki, adding some of the hyperkinetic action of John Woo's heroic bloodletting sagas, and mixing in some of Takeshi Kitano's grim amorality, Takashi Miike added his own extreme tendencies and became a revolutionary filmmaker in Japan. *Dead or Alive* is one of the best of his many films about the relationship between the yakuza and the Chinese triads, but be warned: like almost all his movies, its violence and sexual content are extreme even by modern crime film standards.

5. The Man Who Wasn't There (2001, USA; Joel Coen, dir.)

The Coen brothers had dabbled in all sorts of crime films before: the neo-noir, the murder mystery, the gangster film, and even an inverted shaggy-dog hard-boiled detective story. But this take on the classic noir is one of their greatest triumphs. Joel and Ethan manage to both reduce the stakes and expand the horizons of the genre, and get a terrific performance out of none other than James Gandolfini as a very different kind of heavy.

THE GRIFTERS' UNDERWORLD FAMILY DYNAMICS

No one was better at reveling in the seamy side of noir than the novelist Jim Thompson. The prolific pulp writer created many memorable characters, brought the stylish prose of the hard-boiled mystery forward into a new generation, and most especially, pulled no punches when it came to matters of sex and violence. Although his books have been frequently adapted for the big screen (*The Getaway* and *The Killer Inside Me* made it to Hollywood twice), they've rarely been successful—and, given his very frank approach to the psychosexual kinks of his criminals and killers, Hollywood's moral codes left Thompson's best work unadapted during his most prolific period.

It was not until more than a decade after his death that the best big-screen adaptation of Thompson's work would reach audiences. Released in 1990, *The Grifters* was an all-star production: besides three stunning performances in the lead roles by John Cusack, Anjelica Huston, and Annette Bening, the adaptation was written by Donald E. Westlake, himself a master of the pulp fiction antihero; it was directed by multigenre jack-of-all-trades Stephen Frears; and the movie's highly stylized look was no accident, as the executive producer was none other than Martin Scorsese.

Scorsese's pervasive influence isn't the only way in which *The Grifters* presages *The Sopranos*. The story of small-time con artist Roy Dillon focuses on an aspect of fraud rarely seen in the big leagues of organized crime, but the bloody repercussions that follow when he hooks up with the gorgeous, vulpine long-con operator Myra Langtry (Bening), whose ambitions push him forward into new and frightening directions, is familiar to anyone who's seen how much it costs Tony when he gets in over his head for a payoff. And while *The Grifters* isn't a mob epic, we catch a glimpse of the brute power of big crime: Roy's mother, Lily, herself a career criminal, works for a mobster named Bobo Justus. Played with terrifying understatement by Pat Hingle, Bobo illustrates the true terror behind organized violence; it doesn't even need to do anything to get what it wants. A few threatening words, a few hints of the cost of disobedience, are enough.

But it is especially in its twisted family dynamic that *The Grifters* most predicts the dysfunctional relationships of *The Sopranos*. As toxic as the bond between Tony and Livia may have been, at least it was never as incestuous as that of Roy and Lily—though it's easy to see Livia making the same fatal choice that Lily makes at the gory end of *The Grifters*. And Dr. Melfi would certainly have something to say about how Roy chose a woman so strikingly similar to his manipulative mother. Physically and emotionally, Myra so resembles Lily that the two instantly loathe one another—and their battle over Roy isn't that of two women who sincerely love the same man, but two vicious hoods fighting over the same territory. It's a struggle that would echo in Tony's relationships with his mother and his mistresses.

GET SHORTY AND MOB META-MOVIES

When Elmore Leonard penned the comic crime novel *Get Shorty* in 1990, the idea that the mob had become a self-aware entity was well established. Presaging the way the characters in *The Sopranos* would endlessly watch *GoodFellas* and *The Godfather*, the Mafiosi of the 1970s and 1980s fussed over their depiction in popular culture, and Gambino family boss John Gotti, with his expensive suits and fancy cars, developed a reputation as the first godfather of the media age. But when the film version of *Get Shorty* was released in 1995, it represented something new: it wasn't just a mob movie, but a mob *meta*-movie; not only were the characters aware of their status in pop culture, but the movie was specifically made as a movie aware of the tropes of the gangster picture and willing to have a little fun with them. Rarely had so many disparate elements come together to present an image of the crime film that goofed around with what it had been—and hinted at what it would become.

Get Shorty tells the tale of a Miami loan shark named Chili Palmer (breezily portrayed by John Travolta in high post–*Pulp Fiction* spirits) who, on his way to collect a debt in Las Vegas, is sidetracked into chasing down a dissolute Hollywood producer. Chili, a film buff whose media self-awareness both predates and outstrips Christopher Moltisanti's, decides that while he's got the producer in the palm of his hand, he'll pitch his own idea for a movie—one based on his own life story. Surprisingly, the producer bites; even more surprisingly, it sets off a bidding war with another loan shark, the menacing Bo Catlett (the always excellent Delroy Lindo). Complications ensue.

On the way to its conclusion—which gives plenty a knowing wink to fans of meta-movies—what makes *Get Shorty* so enjoyable is how deftly it handles both the action and thrills of a crime drama and the punchy, unexpected rhythms of a comedy. Much of this is due to its excellent cast and crew. Director Barry Sonnenfeld, before he moved on to big-time blockbusters, had been the cinematographer for the Coen brothers and learned a few things from them about blending comedy and crime. Travolta and Lindo are joined by a great supporting cast, including the consummately professional Gene Hackman, Danny DeVito in the title role, and Dennis Farina as Palmer's rival. Catlett's partner Bear, who plays a key role in the film's denouement, is played by none other than James Gandolfini, four years before his debut as Tony Soprano.

Crime comedies, and mob comedies in particular, tend to be a pretty dreary lot, but Sonnenfeld and his crew, given such a prime piece of source material, turn in a lively, entertaining example of how to do it right. Elmore Leonard is perfect for this sort of project. (And note that in 2010, the FX crime drama *Justified*—based on a Leonard short story and starring *Deadwood* veteran Timothy Olyphant, and strongly influenced by *The Sopranos'* serial narrative revolution—debuted to universal praise.)

QUENTIN TARANTINO, THE FIRST CRIME FILM POSTMODERNIST

When Quentin Tarantino, a self-educated former video store clerk, burst onto the Hollywood scene—first as the screenwriter for movies like *True Romance* and *Natural Born Killers*, and then as a director of films like *Reservoir Dogs* and the breakout success *Pulp Fiction*—he was the victim of the hoary accusation, often hurled at filmmakers with a great deal of visual panache, that he was "all style and no substance." The charge was misguided. While there's no doubt an element of glibness to Tarantino's films, and while he doesn't possess the depth of an Ingmar Bergman, his later films in particular would display an emotional sensibility that showed growing maturity and the skill of a truly great filmmaker.

The accusations of flashiness weren't entirely unjustified, though; and at the very least, it must be admitted that Tarantino brought them on himself. He is the first great crime-movie postmodernist, a pop culture junkie of the highest order, who gathers up every bit of entertainment he's ever seen, sticks them all into a high-speed blender, and splashes the result artfully on screen. Every filmmaker borrows elements from the people who have come before, picking out the pieces they find most effective and incorporating them into their own work. Tarantino, however, doesn't just borrow from some of the movies he likes—he borrows from *all* of them, and is none too subtle about it, either. Film buffs sometimes treat his films—the *Kill Bill* series in particular—as a catalog of set pieces mined from cult films Tarantino has enjoyed. There's a thin line between loving homage and outright thievery, and he walks it more closely than anyone. Sometimes *too* closely.

But Tarantino's talent manages to outshine his own worst tendencies. Even his most self-defeating comments in interviews can't get in the way of the fact that he's an extremely talented filmmaker; his mastery of simply composed shots that play up the emotional reactions between two people is as breathtaking (for those who look closely enough) as his flashy cut scenes and complex chronologies. His having borrowed ideas, characters, and scenes from the movies he grew up watching doesn't erase the sense that he has created a daring new genre of crime films. Even after nearly twenty years, *Pulp Fiction* reads as a strikingly original piece of work, and no amount of imitation found in Tarantino's films can rival the degree to which he was ripped off in the years following its release. The man who watched a thousand movies became the director who launched a hundred imitators.

Tarantino's postmodernist approach may not have an immediately noticeable impact on *The Sopranos*. Tony and his crew undoubtedly would find him an effete poseur, though Christopher would certainly have cited him as an influence on his own attempt at a movie, *Cleaver*. But his impact shows in subtler ways, in how some of the shots are set up, in the show's sense of self-awareness, and especially in the way music blends with on-screen action. The Sopranos may not know it, but they live in Tarantino's postmodern world.

THE LIMEY'S VENGEFUL ANTIHERO

A large part of the allure of crime films is that their villains appeal to a dark tendency in viewers. Their status as outlaws, men outside of decent society, makes them bad guys, but it also allows them to do things we often wish *we* could do, if not for the constraints of that same society. Villains alone can respond to the daily humiliations of life with ego-pleasing vengefulness; they put people in their place who deserve it. They are our bogeymen, but they are also our spirits of vengeance. Dramatists since antiquity have known this, but only in recent years has it become widely acceptable to openly root for the bad guy.

We enjoy the sense of sweet release that comes from stepping outside of normal boundaries and restraints, but ironically, for these antiheroes, that freedom also becomes a prison. Once they're used to using violence and committing crimes to get what they want, they learn that it is the only way they can operate effectively, and that prevents them from ever becoming members of that society they so long spurned—no matter how noble or selfless their goals may be. A moving and brilliant example of this can be found in Steven Soderbergh's *The Limey*, a structurally cunning and magnificently acted modern noir that appeared the same year as the first season of *The Sopranos*.

The powerful British actor Terence Stamp plays Wilson, an aging career criminal just released from another long stint in prison, as playful but full of deadly intensity. He learns that his daughter has died in an auto accident, but, unwilling to accept the official reports of her death, infiltrates the Los Angeles underworld to find out what really happened to her. This brings him into conflict with Peter Fonda, wonderfully inhabiting the role of a music industry bigwig whose soul is still stuck in the '60s, but who supports his extravagant '90s lifestyle by dabbling in the drug market. Wilson learns more than he'd ever suspected, and despite knowing that his daughter desperately wanted him to go straight, he's drawn back into a lifestyle of brutality and revenge.

The Limey is one of Soderbergh's best movies and a classic modern noir. Its clever structure and involving time sequences (some of which employ a fascinating tactic: using material from Stamp's older movies for flashback sequences) are evidence of his skill as a director, and Stamp and Fonda are joined by Lesley Ann Warren, Luis Guzmán, and Nicky Katt in delivering top-rate performances. Lem Dobbs' script is incredible, full of great dialogue and characterization; the audio commentary, in which he and Soderbergh describe their memorable clashes over what form the movie would ultimately take, is highly recommended. And Stamp's adventures in a tawdry, degraded underworld and the clash between his desires to go straight and to do what needs to be done make him a figure just as tragic and doomed as Tony Soprano.

ANALYZE THIS,
COMEDIC MIRROR OF *THE SOPRANOS*

Nothing drives a writer to distraction more than being accused of ripping off someone else's idea. Writers, after all, tend to be a creative and culturally aware lot—that two clever ones could follow the development of a particular new story or social trend and come up with a similar twist on it at the exact same time is not outside the realm of possibility. Ideas emerge simultaneously not because writers poach each other's work, but because they do keep their ideas secret (often out of fear of having their work poached). That's what makes the parallel development of *Analyze This* and *The Sopranos* so odd.

Analyze This is a comedy directed by Second City veteran and *Ghostbusters* writer and actor Harold Ramis and starring Robert De Niro and Billy Crystal. It tells the story of gangster Paul Vitti (De Niro), a longtime Mafioso stressed out over the decline of organized crime, the rising threat of Russian and Asian gangs, betrayals by compatriots turned informant, and his own family issues and sexual peccadilloes. He decides to seek the expertise of a psychiatrist (Crystal) when he's stricken with a crippling panic attack at an inconvenient moment. The psychiatrist has to balance his desire to help his patient with his uncertainty about the man's criminal background and his own culpability in it. The movie was released on March 5, 1999.

Sound familiar? It should. Though *Analyze This* was played almost entirely for laughs, its plot and structure are almost identical to that of *The Sopranos*, which debuted only two months prior. Of course, *The Sopranos* had been in development for more than two years —but then, so had *Analyze This*. Endless speculation was devoted to who had ripped off whom, but the creators on both sides chalked it up to one of those curious coincidences, where two writers develop a similar idea at more or less the same time and, thanks to the vagaries of the production process, both stories come out in close vicinity to one another. Neither director seems to have been aware of the other's work until both were set for a release date, at which time nothing could have been done without incurring unnecessary costs. (Even more curious is the fact that neither work was actually the first to arrive at the concept: in 1997, a *National Lampoon* movie called *The Don's Analyst*, with an almost identical plot and theme, debuted to little fanfare—so little that it was likely not seen by anyone involved with the other two productions.)

Questions of originality aside, *Analyze This* was a popular film and went on to spawn a sequel and a few overseas remakes. The original is flawed, but is the best of the lot; the follow-up, *Analyze That*, was uninspired and dull. The movie didn't become a cultural bellwether as did David Chase's show, and it had the ignominious honor of initiating a rather dreary period in Robert De Niro's career. But it's a decent enough film on its own and a curious exhibit in the history of coincidental Hollywood trends.

Kyle MacLachlan in *Twin Peaks*. (ABC/Photofest)

7

FAITH, FORTITUDE, AND FAMILY: SERIAL TELEVISION PRE-TONY

PROFIT

When *The Sopranos* debuted, it faced a thorny problem: how do you get audiences to tune in week after week to a show whose main character is an immoral, unremorseful killer? How do you maintain a fan base for a show whose protagonists are forever engaged in loathsome behavior? As much as people like to root for the bad guy, there are limits, and no one wants an audience composed entirely of sociopaths. This is one reason there have rarely been shows in which the villain is the hero: while roguish elements are appealing in a protagonist, all it takes is one step too far and audiences will abandon him in a heartbeat. Besides, if the hero is a villain, who is the villain? Whom do audiences root against if the person they're rooting for is doing all the things that normally fall to the bad guy? Why sympathize with a moral monster?

It was a tight balancing act, particularly for David Chase, who was at heart a moralist. He wasn't telling the tale of Tony Soprano because he was some kind of ethical relativist who genuinely found Tony's behavior excusable—far from it. He was presenting audiences with a modern-day morality play, and sometimes became frustrated with viewers' positive reactions to Tony's mayhem. As a filmmaker, he is in the tradition of Lars von Trier and Michael Haneke, two European directors who often spell out their moral lessons by inverting or reversing expected roles and situations. They specialize in locating the unexamined premises underneath standard Hollywood stories and confronting audiences with their ultimate implications. Likewise, Chase was trying to show us not only the high moral cost of a mobster's crimes, but also the price paid by those who sympathize with him and excuse his actions to their own benefit.

Insofar as Chase was successful, he owes a lot to a Fox network drama from 1996 called *Profit*. The debt might seem rather remote, considering the circumstances: *Profit*, while critically acclaimed and widely talked about, suffered from low ratings and not only didn't make it past a single season, but didn't even get to air all eight episodes of its brief run. Many writers have retroactively named it one of the foremost brilliant but canceled series, a great program cut down by the network before it had a chance to truly develop. There is no evidence that David Chase or any of his staff ever saw an episode of *Profit*, and the shows shared no cast members. So regardless of its critical assessment, how much impact could a show that aired for all of five weeks have possibly had on *The Sopranos*? More than you might imagine. ☞

SUPPORTING EVIDENCE: 5 MORE ESSENTIAL ANTECEDENTS

1. *The Prisoner* (1967–1968, UK; George Markstein and Patrick Mc-Goohan, creators)
Though unrelated to the crime drama—its story revolved around an ex-spy, played by co-creator Patrick McGoohan, who retires from service only to be kidnapped and transported to a mysterious island—*The Prisoner* is a powerful antecedent to *The Sopranos*, as well as a spectacular series in its own right. It was one of the very first television programs to break with the episodic tradition, building in story lines and complex backgrounds that would only pay off for attentive viewers.

2. *Police Squad!* (1982, USA; Jim Abrahams and David and Jerry Zucker, creators)
Though it lasted for only six episodes, this lunatic parody of the police procedural/crime drama genre, from the anything-for-a-laugh crew responsible for *Airplane!*, had a huge impact and spawned several movie

sequels. It has no consistency or coherence at all (in fact, that's one of its running jokes), but after a steady diet of gruesome criminal mayhem, it's a welcome relief.

3. *The Singing Detective* (1986, UK; Dennis Potter, creator)

Forget the mediocre 2003 movie remake: the original BBC miniseries is one of the greatest television series of all time. A stunning blend of film noir, human drama, musical fantasy, and postmodern deconstruction, it also serves as a brilliant autobiography—albeit a veiled one—of creator Dennis Potter.

4. *The Untouchables* (1987, USA; Brian De Palma, dir.)

Though both are drawn from identical source material, De Palma's mobster drama couldn't be more different from the television series of the same name. His stellar direction and a rich performance by Robert De Niro as original gangster Al Capone are just two of the qualities that make *The Untouchables* a classic.

5. *La Femme Nikita* (1997–2001, USA; Joel Surnow, creator)

The first TV series based on a thrilling French film of the same name (another would follow in 2010), *La Femme Nikita* is problematic; its plots could be bog-standard, it was frequently artless, and its lead actress, Peta Wilson, was easy on the eye but not a great performer. Still, the story of a violent criminal retrained by the government to be a spy and assassin is notable for its early manifestation of long-term plots, recurring characters, and a strong "mythology."

Quite simply, *Profit* took the notion of the villain as hero further than it had ever been taken on network television. It presented audiences with a protagonist more conniving, more calculating, and more terrifying than any antagonist, and then demanded their sympathy for him. As portrayed with malevolent charm by the handsome, enigmatic young Adrian Pasdar, Jim Profit works a sinister magic on everyone around him. He lies, manipulates, blackmails, and cheats, all the while mouthing platitudes that sound like they come from a management consulting handbook. He spouts positive clichés about making the world a better place, embracing adversity, and living with one's choices, and the whole time he is plotting to destroy everyone around him. Creators David Greenwalt and John McNamara also hit upon the brilliant ploy of having Profit address the audience directly, via voice-over narration, thus implicating them intimately in his criminal worldview—even as he spews out cornball self-help affirmations about how "only three things really matter: your faith, your fortitude, and your family."

Profit is the story of a ruthless young corporate climber determined to rise from his position in the auditing department of a huge multinational conglomerate as high as his ambition and willpower will take him. The very first time we see Jim Profit, he's blackmailing the secretary of a dead executive—at the man's funeral. He only gets worse from there: Profit shows himself to be a swindler, a liar, a forger, an extortionist, a cuckolder, and a thief, all within the first two episodes. He's in a semi-incestuous relationship with his stepmother (originally, it was even worse—in early drafts of the script, it was his biological mother, before the network asked the creators to tone it down), who is blackmailing him in turn by threatening to reveal his true past. He spends his nights half naked in front of a computer, his normally perfect hair disheveled and wild, literally exploding the online icons of his rivals as he systematically destroys their careers.

Profit, it is revealed, was raised by a brutal, abusive father (the details of the story were lifted by Greenwalt and McNamara from the history of a real serial killer) and will now stop at nothing, not even murder, to get the one thing he wants: control of Gracen & Gracen Inc. Pasdar gives a terrific performance. It's the kind of acting that would completely steal the show if he were the featured villain on a more traditional program, but *Profit* is infinitely more subversive because this bad guy is meant to be the hero. Pasdar is also the beneficiary of some truly chilling scripts—the pilot ends with the unforgettable image of Jim Profit sleeping nude in a decrepit shipping box, a constant reminder of his traumatic childhood.

The show takes huge risks from its very first moments. Not only must it show Profit in a bad enough light to establish that he is the villain, but it also must also keep us involved enough in his character that we continue to want him to thrive. In most traditional hero-villain stories, we are guaranteed that the hero will find some way to win; after all, the bad guy only has to win once, and he'll kill the good guy, thus ending the story. *Profit* must take the opposite tack: one single mistake for Jim Profit and his machinations are exposed, his evil plans laid bare, and his position, his freedom, and possibly his life are forfeit. He must not only be clever, but lucky. His story plays with this concept from the very beginning: it looks as though he'll be caught in the first episode, thanks to G&G executive Jack Walters and the company's determined security chief, Joanne Meltzer, but Profit engineers a reversal of fortune and comes out on top through a series of well-deployed blackmail schemes. Meltzer (nicely played by Lisa Zane, whose performance suggests more than a little that the character is afflicted with her own psychological problems) becomes Profit's archenemy, but is never quite able to pin him down as the architect of his many evils. In this way, *Profit* keeps us engaged with Pasdar's enticing wickedness but dangles the possibility of justice before us almost like a threat. This, in particular, is a device that David Chase later mastered. It may create a difficult moral situation and present some problems for writers, but keeping your main character looking down the barrel of a gun makes for some high-stakes drama.

David Greenwalt would go on to become one of the movers and shakers behind *Buffy the Vampire Slayer*, another early adopter of the season-long narrative storytelling approach that would characterize *The Sopranos* and revolutionize television. He was inspired to create *Profit* after taking in a performance of William Shakespeare's *Richard III*—specifically, one starring Ian McKellen in the title role, with the setting updated to an alternate fascist England of the 1930s. (The play would be made into an outstanding movie in 1995, just a year before *Profit* premiered.) It's easy to spot the origins of the story: while *Profit* lacks the Shakespearean structure of, say, *Deadwood*, its main character is a perfect incarnation of the villainous King Richard. Profit shares the monarch's uncanny ability to read situations and turn them to his advantage, and even more so, his talent for making allies out of his worst enemies—taking people who by all rights should loathe him for the chaos he rains on them and turning them into his abettors and accomplices. The two characters also possess a Machiavellian ability to manipulate people and a bizarre charm: though Profit, handsome and soft-spoken, lacks Richard's physical deformation, both are able to so effectively control people around them that no one thinks of either as an enemy. As Greenwalt and McNamara would centuries later, Shakespeare felt it was a challenge to present such a malevolent creature as the main character of a story; unfortunately, circumstances prohibited audiences from finding out whether Jim Profit, like Richard III, would ultimately be made to pay the price for his evil ways.

Profit's sins would only become more monstrous as the show progressed. Had it not been canceled prematurely, the creators explain on the DVD commentary, his schemes would have become even more ambitious, encompassing poisoning, murder, and even terrorism. But another clever trick helped take the stink off of him: the show's setting in a competitive corporate environment. No one was entirely blameless in the world of *Profit*: the main character's blackmail victims were trying to cover up heinous deeds of their own, and his targets were mercenary, greedy, deeply corrupt businessmen and women. The people he targeted were adulterers, embezzlers, and cheats; the Gracen family itself was stocked with drunks, brutes, and creeps. Following in the path of the prime-time soap opera *Dallas*, *Profit* succeeded at least partly by serving, at the height of the prosperous Clinton '90s, as a satire on corporate greed and big-business venality. *The Sopranos* would also pick up this trail, portraying many of Tony's victims as being just as bad as or worse than he was, which only served to net audiences into his own self-deception.

Unfortunately, this proved part of the downfall of *Profit* as well as part of its appeal. The world of business was portrayed as so corrupt and vicious that it raised eyebrows in that community. Editorials in *Fortune* and *The Wall Street Journal* wagged scolding fingers at the satire, and Fox network head Rupert Murdoch—himself a rather cutthroat corporate titan—was rumored to be a detractor. Ratings aside, the vox populi also had a problem with *Profit*. By the time of *The Sopranos*, the villain-as-hero was a bit more established and didn't strike American taste buds as quite so sour. But in 1996, it was still a very controversial concept, and many viewers, especially conservatives and the religious, were scandalized by a weekly drama focused on the misdeeds of an incestuous, murderous sociopath stabbing his way up the corporate ladder. Their disapprobation, combined with low ratings and some ill will from network executives, doomed *Profit* to an early end.

Even after such a demise, though, the damage had been done. *Profit* was done for (and a plan to resurrect the character of Jim Profit on the *Buffy the Vampire Slayer* spin-off *Angel* never came to fruition), but its name was constantly revived as an example of a show canceled too soon. The critics had loved it, and its gleefully amoral approach was one of the reasons why. It was edgy, daring, and subversive, a complete change of pace from the bog-standard morality plays of most television dramas. Its intricate plotting impressed reviewers and was an early warning sign of the shift to long-form serial narrative arcs in TV drama; its willingness to push at the medium's moral boundaries was cutting-edge; and it proved to be a telling bellwether of the time, with relevant plots, a high-tech sensibility, and a conception of the antihero that went beyond anything networks had been willing to tolerate before. For *The Sopranos*, it represented a little seen but inestimably important predecessor to the way Tony would be depicted.

THE UNTOUCHABLES AND GANGSTER TELEVISION

Crime shows have been a staple of American television since the early days of low-wattage black-and-white sets. A number of factors, however—censorship from network standards and practices departments, social pressures, expedience, convenience, tradition, simplicity, and the ever-present fear of litigation—conspired to keep most early crime shows in the mode of police procedurals, straightforward cop shows, and the occasional noir-tinged hard-boiled detective drama. The mob epic was not yet a staple of the motion picture industry, J. Edgar Hoover was still denying the significance and even the existence of the Mafia, and many organized crime figures were still alive and well, and equipped with a phalanx of bloodthirsty lawyers. So for much of television's first few decades, the mob was a minimal presence in narrative series.

The first program to break that barrier, and to prominently feature gangsters as recurring characters, was a half-hour ABC cop show called *The Lawless Years*. Set during the rowdy mobster era of Prohibition, it starred James Gregory as a tough New York cop and drew some of its plots and characters from real-world events. Much more successful, however—and more prominent when it comes to tracing the path of *The Sopranos* through television history—was an hour-long police drama that debuted only six months later on the same network. *The Untouchables* starred Robert Stack as real-life federal agent Eliot Ness and was based on Ness' memoir about fighting gangsters in Prohibition-era Chicago. Using the book as a springboard, the show colorfully portrayed many of the great villains of the period, often by playing a bit loose with the facts. Aside from Ness and his incorruptible crew, recurring characters included Al Capone, Frank Nitti, Bugs Moran, and Ma Barker.

The Untouchables ran for four seasons and proved a commercial success, thanks to its stylish presentation, excellent acting, jazzy score (by Nelson Riddle and Pete Rugolo), and memorable narration. It also marked early television appearances by a number of future Hollywood stars just getting their start in entertainment: future *Godfather* stars James Caan and Robert Duvall both had roles on the show, as did a young Robert Loggia, decades from his appearance on *The Sopranos*. *The Untouchables* also demonstrated the risks of making a Mafia show, then as now: it was protested by prominent Italian-Americans, Frank Sinatra among them, for stereotyping their ethnicity as hoodlums and criminals, and was sued by the family of Al Capone, who objected to the use of their famous relative on a profitable TV show without their permission.

Mob stories would come and go many times in subsequent years, but none achieved the success of *The Untouchables* until the late 1980s, when a pair of series—CBS's *Wiseguy*, which featured the then-new device of multi-episode story arcs, and NBC's *Crime Story*, a period drama featuring a Mafia hood as one of its main characters—appeared and used some of the techniques that would presage *The Sopranos*. It wouldn't be long before the organized crime drama became a television staple.

DALLAS AND THE PRIME-TIME SOAPS

Serial storytelling in American television isn't exactly a new development. In fact, while we've come to think of the episodic program as the norm, serial narratives have dominated daytime television since the 1950s, in the form of the soap opera. The genre was so named because advertisers—especially manufacturers of household goods like soaps and detergents—knew they could count on repeat business; thanks to the ongoing narrative, housewives would tune in day after day. And indeed, the form proved highly successful and extremely addictive. But for many years, it remained in the realm of daytime television, and was considered off-limits for prime time, the network's key piece of real estate.

That began to change in the late 1970s, particularly with the debut of the hugely successful *Dallas*. Beginning as a miniseries in 1978, the show proved a gigantic hit and ran for thirteen seasons, triggering many imitators and making prime time safe for the soap opera format. The story of the lives and loves of a family of Texas oil billionaires, *Dallas* took a few liberties with the soap opera format that would become standard for prime-time serial dramas: single-camera setups, lots of location shooting, multiple story arcs, and end-of-season cliffhangers. The stories of romance, betrayal, deception, and greed stayed intact, but clever new storytelling tricks were brought in to expand the viewing demographic to include men as well as women, and single people as well as housewives. But perhaps the greatest trick, made manifest in *Dallas'* breakaway star Larry Hagman as the Machiavellian schemer J. R. Ewing, was one that crime dramas had learned long ago: give the audiences someone to hate.

A juicy villain has always been the key to crime films, and soap operas, too, knew the value of a recurring character whom audiences would tune in over and over again to boo and hiss. But most television crime shows, limited by network standards or tradition, kept the focus on the good guys, only occasionally bringing back a recurring villain and keeping the stories distinctly in the episodic mode. It was prime-time soap operas that gave us figures like J. R.—conniving, cruel, morally shady, yet endlessly watchable and curiously identifiable—and paved the way for a new world where a show's protagonist and primary villain were one in the same. It was this development, more than any other, that would pave the way for *The Sopranos*.

Like any other highly successful show, *Dallas* spawned endless imitations, spin-offs and rip-offs, the most successful of which were *Dynasty*, *Falcon Crest* and *Knots Landing*. After they burned out in the late 1990s, a new generation (including *Beverly Hills 90210* and *Melrose Place*) appeared in their wake, but the key development was the appearance of the serial narrative models in other genres: soon enough, the soap opera model, with its multi-episode story arcs and recurring antiheroes, would begin to populate police procedurals, medical dramas, and other types of programs previously harnessed to the episodic model. This shift would soon prove groundbreaking.

HBO, THE MOVIE CHANNEL THAT CHANGED TELEVISION

As befits its original name—the initials stand for Home Box Office—HBO began as a movie channel. Evolving from early experiments in cable and satellite television, HBO officially came into being in 1972, picking up its subscriber base by broadcasting sports and commercial-free movies. Its position as a cable channel allowed it to avoid the kind of censorship imposed by broadcast network standards and practices, and its subscription model allowed it to do away with commercials. By the time it went to 24-hour-a-day broadcasting in 1981, its appeal to most viewers was as a place to see first-run movies, uncut, uncensored, and uninterrupted, only months after they'd played in theaters. Back then, few suspected a channel known for showing films would eventually play such a huge role in transforming television.

Original programming was nothing new to HBO; it featured stand-up comedy, variety shows, and sports series as early as the mid-1970s. It delved into narrative programming in the early '80s with children's programming (the beloved *Fraggle Rock*), and with sitcoms and anthology programs that took advantage of the fact that the network could feature nudity and adult language, though few of those were big successes to begin with. The first show that signaled what HBO's original programming would ultimately become was the 1988 miniseries *Tanner '88*. Its overarching narrative, sophisticated storytelling, and high-profile creators (including director Robert Altman and writer Garry Trudeau, famous for his *Doonesbury* comic strip) garnered a lot of critical attention and established HBO's reputation as a go-to location for high-quality television.

HBO forsook serial drama for most of the '90s, focusing on sports and comedy series. But 1997's *Oz*, an intense prison drama, was the beginning of a wave of original dramas that won the network dozens of Emmys and set the bar for original narrative programming higher than it had ever been before. *Sex and the City* found a huge audience (albeit an entirely different one), and the floodgates truly opened with the debut of *The Sopranos* in 1999. By this time, HBO was not only able to feature grown-up storytelling, but was also willing to sink more money into its original work, ensuring a constant supply of top-grade creators and visual style that matched the flair of the scripts. *The Sopranos* was followed by other critical smashes like *The Wire*, *Deadwood*, *The Pacific*, *Boardwalk Empire*, and *Treme*.

Once it became clear that serial drama was catnip for critics and fans, other cable networks followed HBO's lead. Showtime produced *The Tudors*, *Weeds*, *Nurse Jackie* (featuring Edie Falco), *Californication*, and *Dexter*, among others; even second-tier movie network Starz got in on the act with its original historical dramas *Spartacus* and *Camelot* and the short-lived cult comedy *Party Down*. It wasn't long before regular cable networks started producing their own original shows—like AMC's *Breaking Bad* and *Mad Men* and the FX Network's *The Shield*, *Sons of Anarchy*, and *Justified*. Eventually, despite the continuing restrictions of network censors, the format would cross over onto the big broadcast channels, and HBO's TV revolution would be complete. Echoes of *The Sopranos* would be heard in the places one would least expect.

TWIN PEAKS AND THE RISE OF AUTEUR TV

At first glance, no two shows seem more different than *Twin Peaks* and *The Sopranos*. Steeped in David Lynch's inimitable mix of intellectual aesthetics, poetic visuals, twisted small-town Americana, and creepy, insinuating surrealism, the 1990 series would appear to be a world apart from David Chase's nervy, visceral, street-level crime drama. But whatever tonal differences exist—and they run less deep than you might imagine—*Twin Peaks* changed television for the better and set the stage for shows like *The Sopranos*, where one person's artistic vision could be carried out in what was once the least auteur-driven of media.

Twin Peaks didn't exactly start as a television series. It rose from the residue of a handful of unfinished projects (including a never-realized Marilyn Monroe biopic) involving the notorious Lynch and his collaborator Mark Frost. But Lynch's agent had pushed him to do television work, and, encouraged to work on an idea inspired by his longtime fascination for the dark corners of the clean-scrubbed small-town psyche, he delivered ABC a bare-bones pitch for a show blending police procedurals with surrealist soap opera. The network took the bait, and one of the strangest shows in television history was born—and would go on to change the culture's notion of what TV was capable of.

Initially focused on the murder of Laura Palmer, a popular teenager in a small lumber town, *Twin Peaks* quickly cast its nets much farther from shore. Frost and Lynch envisioned a sprawling, intricate "mythology" for the show, and this element in particular would prove hugely influential in the future of serial storytelling. They also populated their tiny town with unforgettable characters, from the Log Lady to taciturn Native American tracker Deputy Hawk, all seen through the eyes of an outsider: enthusiastic FBI Agent Dale Cooper, played by Kyle MacLachlan. Though the creators both burned out in the second season, after the story's central mystery was solved, along the way they set a stunning precedent for what television could be when overseen by showrunners deeply involved in the creative process: at its best, *Twin Peaks* was beautiful, strange, funny, disturbing, and emotionally engaging—and, most important to the network, it encouraged viewers to tune in week after week, lest they miss an important revelation.

This blend of soap opera storytelling and cinematic scope proved to be a game-changing development in the history of television. From *Twin Peaks* on, ambitious filmmakers began to perceive television not as a hell they'd be relegated to after a few box office failures, but a realm of new and exciting possibilities even movies couldn't match. David Chase was one of the auteurish show creators who arrived in the wake of *Twin Peaks* (and its influence on him can be seen clearly, especially in his reliance on dream sequences to illuminate characters' psychological nuances), and its influence can be seen to this day in shows like *The Walking Dead*.

AMERICAN GOTHIC AND THE VILLAIN AS HERO

Shaun Cassidy used up all his luck in his teens. In the late 1970s, the son of a show business family became a singing superstar with a devoted audience of young girls and also landed a role as a breakout TV actor, starring in *The Hardy Boys Mysteries* when he was only nineteen. He continued to act onstage into the '80s and then decided to begin a career behind the scenes, writing and producing television shows. But apparently, finding huge stardom before he could drink legally depleted his karma, because Cassidy has primarily become known as the producer of a number of shows that, despite their high quality and cult success, never managed to find a popular audience and were canceled after a single season.

The first, and best, of these was *American Gothic*, which debuted in 1995. Created by Cassidy and produced by Sam Raimi, it was unfairly pegged as a *Twin Peaks* rip-off due to its evil-in-a-small-town vibe and air of creeping menace. But *American Gothic* was something unique: unlike *Profit*, which would feature a villainous protagonist who adopted a harmless facade, it gave us a main character who was openly sinister and manipulative—and demonstrated that viewers would root for him anyway. It was one of the first of the new wave of serial narratives that would culminate in *The Sopranos*, and one of the first shows where the creators cunningly steered audiences into feeling sympathy for a morally repugnant character.

American Gothic's proto–Tony Soprano was Lucas Buck, played by the delightfully cynical Gary Cole. The profoundly corrupt sheriff of tiny Trinity, South Carolina, Buck—who it is suggested might be the devil himself—rules the town with an iron fist. The crimes of his past, though, literally come back to haunt him: a young boy named Caleb—the offspring of a woman Buck had raped—poses a metaphysical threat to his unquestioned rule, and the boy is aided by the ghost of his older sister, murdered by Buck. Externals forces as well as internal threats conspire to unseat Sheriff Buck, but at no time in the series is there any question that he is the central character; and he's so charismatic and likable, even when doing the foulest deeds, that Cassidy and his writers have us pulling for him to succeed even when we're aware of the destructive consequences of his actions.

This approach would find its zenith with the appearance of Tony Soprano in 1999, but Cassidy wasn't quite done with it yet. He put forth a similar scenario in 2005 with *Invasion*, a gorgeously filmed, brilliantly written serial mystery in the style of *Lost*. In the show, a hurricane in a small Florida town has masked an invasion by alien creatures, who took over the personalities and bodies of locals. This time, the reliable William Fichtner played the manipulative and secretive sheriff who will do anything to keep control of his community—but as with *American Gothic*, bad luck and low ratings led to the show's cancellation after only one season.

Jon Hamm in *Mad Men*. (AMC/Photofest)

8

LISTEN TO THE THUNDER:
SERIAL TELEVISION POST-TONY

DEADWOOD

Wedged completely within the series run of *The Sopranos*—
its thirty-six episodes ran from 2004 to 2006—appeared a show
that took the great promise of David Chase's show and inverted
it, turned it inward, and, ironically, expanded on it. *Deadwood*, a
brilliantly written and acted story about the development of the
notoriously lawless Wild West town in what would later become
South Dakota, was a show that shared almost every concern of
The Sopranos, but twisted them inside out—telling a story about the
building of communities and relationships that would be well on
their way to disintegrating by the time Tony and his crew came
along. It gave those concerns new avenues of perspective, as well,
delivering a voice and a viewpoint to characters Chase's series
tended to marginalize or exclude. *Deadwood* couldn't possibly have
existed without *The Sopranos*, but in its three short seasons, it told a
story far more ambitious and complex than its inspiration managed
in twice that time.

As in *The Sopranos*, the character at the center of *Deadwood*—the
show and the town—is a morally corrupted man, no stranger to
brutality and violence, and not above committing murder to get
what he wants. Al Swearengen (played by the British actor Ian Mc-
Shane, in the performance of a lifetime) is the owner of the Gem
Saloon. Like Tony, he makes his money off of whoring, gambling,
and arranging protection and other resources for the criminals and
thugs of the Dakota territory; his clientele are the gold miners, In-

dian hunters, and other ne'er-do-wells who pass through the town on their search for easy riches. But Al's primary fear isn't the law—Deadwood has none. Al knows how to game the system, and even from the beginning he knows that the law is coming to Deadwood; his concern isn't avoiding it, but arranging it to suit his own purposes. In an unexpected but brilliant inversion of the standard crime drama, the people who most threaten Swearengen's plans are the police and the government—not because they seek to shut down his illegal activities, but because they are far more able to make a profit off of those activities than he is.

Swearengen isn't a traditional antihero; he's an unrepentant, savage killer who's not above plotting the murder of an innocent, traumatized young girl to cover his tracks. But *Deadwood* pulls off one of the most stunning reversals in television history with his character arc: beginning the show as a malevolent murderer willing to kill anyone who stands in his way, he ends it as something of the town patriarch, protecting a woman he once tried to drive out of town against a threat even greater than he himself could pose. Al is initially threatened by the arrival of the morally upstanding former sheriff Seth Bullock (played at a constant slow boil by Timothy Olyphant) and his new friend, the legendary gunfighter Wild Bill Hickok; but he is astute enough to realize that the best way to take care of Bullock isn't to destroy him, but to convince him that protecting the interests of the town means forging an alliance against outsiders. Where Tony Soprano sees himself as a perpetual outsider, forever on the fringes of the system while reaping its benefits, Al Swearengen walks a fine line, slowly edging his town into the modern world while making sure he benefits from every move that's made.

Tony's enemies are federal law enforcement agents *and* members of his own crew, driven by greed, divided loyalties, and in some cases a desire to cooperate with the law rather than face a prison sentence. Al's crew, on the other hand, while subject to the common temptations of avarice and jealousy, are generally quite loyal and unafraid of what law there is. The government represents the enemy in *Deadwood* not only because it is corrupt and crooked, but also because it can take away the source of Al's power and wealth: it can turn the land over to the Sioux Indians, mooting all the land claims of the businessmen and gold miners; it can cede the town to a territory in which Al has no political sway; or it can turn the whole issue over to the military, whose brute force makes his sinister power look puny. The greatest villain of the series isn't Al or his hatefully misogynist rival Cy Tolliver (a furious, explosive Powers Boothe) or the Indians or the bought-off politicians or any of the thugs, killers, and scum that drift through Deadwood. It's the fantastically wealthy businessman George Hearst, played by Gerald McRaney, who comes to buy up the whole town for its gold riches. The nature of Hearst's evil isn't so much that he's a remorseless killer or an amoral monster, but that he simply plays the game better, and on a higher level, than anyone else.

This is just one of many ways *Deadwood* cleverly flips the script presented by *The Sopranos*. The New Jersey mob operates by virtue of a sort of shadow capitalism, winning its stolen profits from the legitimate work done by others or dealing in trades forbidden by law. *Deadwood* takes law out of the picture and shows how Al and his gang make money from the absolutely unrestricted operation of the market. Tony bemoans the alleged prejudice against Italians while using it to justify the sort of behavior that reinforces that prejudice, complaining that his criminal predecessors were forced to turn to crime because they were excluded from the American system. But *Deadwood* shows us the Chinese—who experienced bigotry and isolation beyond anything ever suffered by Tony's forefathers—and while they too seek the profits made available to them by criminal enterprises, doing so ironically binds their leader, Mr. Wu (Keone Young), even more tightly to America through his alliance with Swearengen. Law enforcement in Tony's world often seems as wicked as the Mafia, blackmailing mobsters and their families into turning against one another to avoid prosecution in an endless game of betrayal; *Deadwood* shows us how a morally righteous man like Seth Bullock can ally himself with a man he once considered his worst enemy, once he is convinced that Swearengen is the lesser of two evils.

Deadwood also performs the vital service of giving voice to the voiceless. While union men, whores, and innocent bystanders populate the world of both *The Sopranos* and *Deadwood*, it is the latter that gives them a platform and an outlook. Unions exist in *The Sopranos* to be corrupted; they are a funnel for Tony's ill-gotten gains and a source of no-show jobs for his cronies. In *Deadwood*, they are the only hope for George Hearst's oppressed workers and a target of his Pinkerton agents, who act as a cruel and one-sided police force. The dancers at Tony's Bada Bing club rarely step out of the role of eye candy or easy victim; *Deadwood* never soft-pedals the horrible treatment of the whores at the Gem Saloon and elsewhere, but gives them compelling personalities, rich backstories, and flaws and aspirations of their own. They are still little more than property, but we are never allowed to forget that they are human, and some of them—particularly Paula Malcomson as the steely Trixie and Kim Dickens as the deeply wounded Joanie—are among the show's most fascinating characters. And while David Chase tends to put innocent victims of Mafia power plays on the margins, keeping our focus on the way Tony justifies the violence he visits on them, *Deadwood* makes us feel for them every second. When an innocent person gets caught up in the plans of one or another of the town's power players, we take the emotional brunt like a physical blow. ☞

SUPPORTING EVIDENCE:
5 MORE VITAL POST-*SOPRANOS* PROJECTS

1. *Alias* (2001–2006, USA; J. J. Abrams, creator)
Another project from the ubiquitous J. J. Abrams, *Alias*, like *Lost*, wasn't exactly a crime drama, but it was rife with elements inherited from the post-*Sopranos* television landscape. Beyond that, the constant battles between rival intelligence agencies in this sci-fi-tinged spy drama play up the same razor-thin moral line that separates the cops and criminals in the best gangster films.
2. *Sin City* (2005, USA; Frank Miller, Robert Rodriguez, and Quentin Tarantino, dirs.)

This postmodern pastiche, adapted from several installments of co-director Frank Miller's series of graphic novels, may have been little more than a collection of scraps from various hard-boiled classics of the past. But its incredible visual style and innovative use of color and framing still made it one of the most indelible neo-noirs of the new century.

3. *Rome* (2005–2007, USA; Bruno Heller, William J. MacDonald, and John Milius, creators)

A mini-trend emerged recently aimed at telling historical narratives "*Sopranos*-style"—which, unfortunately, usually just meant with tons of bloodshed, betrayal, and boobs, instead of with psychological depth; *The Tudors*, *Camelot*, and *The Borgias* all fit this mode. The first and best was HBO's *Rome*. Although flawed, and so costly that it was canceled before its time, it is buoyed by excellent performances and vivid location filming.

4. *Life on Mars* (2006–2007, UK; Matthew Graham, Tony Jordan, and Ashley Pharoah, creators)

Forget the inferior U.S. remake and hunt down the original British version of this highly original blend of sci-fi mystery and police procedural. The story of a modern police detective who's injured in a car crash and wakes up in 1973 nicely contrasts the differences between crime dramas of today and the past, and its frequent hallucinations and dream sequences conjure up the haunted world of Tony Soprano.

5. *Gangland* (2007–present, USA)

Like their literary counterparts, true crime documentaries tend to be exploitative affairs, and truthfully, the History Channel's *Gangland* series is guilty of that charge. But for the gangster junkie, its commitment to exploring, however sensationally, every criminal outfit imaginable, from the Mafia to biker gangs to Asian mobsters, can be addictive.

While no one would deny the multifaceted nature of the characters on *The Sopranos*, we generally cannot forget—if for no other reason than that David Chase won't let us—that most of them are bad men engaged in bad behavior. Their moments of redemption are few and far between, and any moral complexity is usually invented to justify their villainy. But *Deadwood* does a superb job of keeping us off of our moral footing. By the end of the series, when the staunch moral champion Bullock has allied himself with the murderous Swearengen against Hearst (who historically showed no evidence of being the demonic figure he is here), no one thinks to blame him. Likewise, the good guys are often far from ideal: Hickok is a bully and a gambling addict, and Bullock is a hotheaded, short-tempered man who rarely thinks things through. Mrs. Alma Garrett, the heir to a vast gold reserve, is arrogant, trapped in a loveless marriage, and dismissive of the good advice of others. When Swearengen tries to drive her out of town, Hickok urges her to "listen to the thunder"—to be aware of the threats gathering around her—because a failure to do so could jeopardize her life and that of her adopted daughter. She ignores his counsel, and the high cost of her independence is paid in blood.

There are many other examples of how *Deadwood* covers much of the same ground as *The Sopranos* but diverges in interesting and unexpected ways. Tony's world may be decaying, but he still lives in a gorgeous house and dresses himself up in thousand-dollar suits when he's not lounging around in a bathrobe; Al's is literally filthy. Suits are stained with blood and worse, the roads are bogged with mud and shit, and you can almost smell how infrequently the people bathe. Tony and his crew may not curse *less* than Al and his gang, but the vulgarity of *Deadwood* is downright Shakespearean—grand and poetic. Since the aesthetic approach of *The Sopranos* is drawn from the operatic traditions of Scorsese and Coppola, its sex scenes are eroticized and its violence highly stylized; both sex and violence in *Deadwood* are nasty, brutish, and short. Even *Deadwood*'s characters' health issues reflect a different universe: Al undergoes an illness in season 2 that seems minor by our standards, but it's shown as infinitely more horrifying and painful (and is far harder to watch) than Tony's recovery from being gut-shot by Uncle Junior.

The creator of *Deadwood* was David Milch—like Chase, a television veteran (he'd most famously worked on the police procedurals *Hill Street Blues* and *NYPD Blue*, both of which were pioneers in prime-time serial storytelling) given a chance to make his dream show. He delegated writing and directing duties to a number of talented professionals—Hollywood legend Walter Hill directed the pilot, and *Sopranos* veterans Alan Taylor and Tim Van Patten each helmed episodes—but like Chase, he oversaw every episode, guiding the overall direction of the show and adding his own distinctive writing voice to every installment. (He is also a hugely entertaining figure, irascible and prickly; the DVD commentaries are a must-hear, with Milch as much of a character as any of the figures on screen.) He was a true showrunner, imprinting his vision for the show on each episode, from its language to its visual style to its uniformly excellent cast. Aside from a few of the lead roles, the actors on *Deadwood* are as far as you can get from Hollywood beautiful people; they are often as ugly and weathered as the moral atmosphere in which they work.

Milch showed one distinct weakness that Chase avoided: he jumped right back into TV production after *Deadwood* was canceled, and the result was the intriguing but badly executed *John from Cincinnati*. But for the three seasons Milch was in charge of HBO's vision of the Wild West, he picked up the gauntlet of *The Sopranos* and met its challenge in an amazingly successful manner that holds up tremendously well. Rumors of a *Deadwood* movie have come and gone, and seem to be little more than pipe dreams, but if all we ever get out of this electrifying historical fiction is the three seasons that exist, that's more than enough to consider it among the greats.

THE WIRE, THE PINNACLE OF CRIME TV

Though its ratings were never as high as those of *The Sopranos* (in fact, it was in dire danger of cancellation prior to its third season), HBO's *The Wire* was the logical culmination of the tone set for sophisticated television storytelling by David Chase and company. Starting just a few years after *The Sopranos* made its debut, the five-season series—a novelistic, brilliantly acted, and stunningly executed crime drama about life on the troubled streets of Baltimore—may be the greatest television series ever made, and is a natural next step for any *Sopranos* fan.

The two shows shared many characteristics: both were ambitious, contemporary urban crime dramas that showed the effect of organized crime on a changing society, and vice versa. Both shared an underrated sense of humor and a phenomenal ensemble cast. But while *The Sopranos* focused largely on the criminals, *The Wire* showed every angle: it hardly had a central character (Dominic West as the brilliant but self-destructive Detective Jimmy McNulty came close, but even he wasn't in a number of episodes), but spread its eye everywhere. Honest cops and crooked ones, well-meaning but misguided crooks and monstrous street thugs, decent politicians and corrupt party hacks, working men and women, the ultra-rich, corner kids, and overtaxed teachers all formed part of what became an intricate tableau of a modern dysfunctional city.

Creator David Simon, a former Baltimore police reporter, chose a group of relative unknowns to populate his interconnected universe of cops and criminals. Among his unforgettable creations: Omar Little, the shotgun-toting Robin Hood of the streets; the ambitious, morally frustrated Mayor Tommy Carcetti; the brutal, savage young drug lord Marlo Stanfield; and the wannabe-tough youngster Namond Brice. These are just a few of the dozens of compelling characters in a fantastically written show, a masterpiece of storytelling in which, as the canny, quiet cop Lester Freamon points out, "every piece matters." From its realistic use of street language to its spectacular dialogue to its profound emotional weight to its ability to tie together disparate story threads with ease, *The Wire* took everything great about *The Sopranos* and elevated it to a level never seen before on television.

Few people actually saw *The Wire* during its original run; it was a constant ratings disappointment, and likely got the fourth and fifth seasons its creators wanted so badly merely as a sop to the hundreds of critics who tried to spread the word of its greatness. But almost everyone who did see it recognized it as a revelation, a television series like no other and a great leap forward in the potential of the medium. It reached few, but influenced everyone it reached. For all its self-evident greatness, though, *The Wire* would likely never have existed without Tony Soprano: the critical goodwill *The Sopranos* brought to HBO gave the show its most vociferous supporters, the audience for smart crime drama that *The Sopranos* helped nurture gave it what followers it had, and money generated from the success of *The Sopranos* helped pay for it.

MAD MEN AND ITS DEBT TO THE SOPRANOS

Of all the projects involving the creative team behind *The Sopranos* since its final episode aired in 2007, few have received as much critical attention as AMC's *Mad Men*. Created by Matthew Weiner, author of a dozen episodes of *The Sopranos* during its final three seasons, *Mad Men* has not earned the kind of ratings that the HBO program did, but it has attracted the attention of nearly every critic in the country and the unvarnished love of a small but influential demographic of viewers, who have made it one of the most talked-about shows of the twenty-first century.

Mad Men tells the story of Don Draper, a Madison Avenue advertising executive in the early 1960s who despite his genius is challenged by a changing industry he may not understand as well as he thinks he does, as well as his own self-destructive tendencies, which stand to jeopardize all that he's worked for. The parallels between Draper and Tony Soprano couldn't be more clear: though the former is a remarkably handsome, dapper, and respectable man and the latter a bullish, brutal criminal, the two are effective leaders paralyzed by their own psychological problems, serial infidelities, and status in a highly competitive field in a dangerous state of flux.

But it's less in the lead role that *Mad Men* resembles *The Sopranos* than it is in the shows' stylistic and formal approach. Weiner's show benefited, as did other critically acclaimed dramas, from the taste for serial storytelling kicked off by *The Sopranos*. Like many HBO shows that popped up in David Chase's wake, it mastered the use of montage to move its story forward in time and bring audiences up to date with major developments in the lives of characters. Most of all, though, *Mad Men* has proven that for a show to truly thrive in the post-*Sopranos* era, it needs to have a solid hook, and more, a sense of style. Just as *The Sopranos* attracted audiences in part because it was such a successful mélange of mob-movie elements, *Mad Men* has won over viewers and critics thanks to its gorgeous sense of style and appealing evocation of the sharp suits, three-martini lunches, and high-stakes meetings of a bygone era of American business. *Mad Men* may play slightly loose with historical verisimilitude, but it is enthralling in its ability to conjure up a vanished world of class and cool.

Though Weiner did good work on *The Sopranos*, he was often inconsistent, and some of his failings—particularly his seeming befuddlement at out-of-the-mainstream subcultures—are picked up in *Mad Men*. But the latter show improves on his previous work in many ways, as well. Roles for women are far richer in *Mad Men* than they were in the male-dominated world of *The Sopranos*. (Weiner also brought along talent from his previous gig, including directors Alan Taylor and Phil Abraham and actress Cara Buono.) He deserves credit for taking solid storytelling lessons and a sophisticated narrative framework from *The Sopranos* and applying them to a stylish and extravagant new model.

SERIAL STORYTELLING COMES TO NETWORK TV

The great leap forward into high-quality serialized storytelling in television was pioneered by HBO with *The Sopranos*. Other cable channels picked up the torch and presented their own dramas featuring novelistic scales and multi-episode plot arcs; it seemed that cable's ability to minimize advertising and present more "adult" situations (that is, situations saturated with sex, violence and strong language) made it a natural for this new kind of TV. Mainstream broadcast networks were selective about expanding the soap opera format, however. There had been some efforts by networks to create shows with long narrative arcs and complex mythologies, but they were largely confined to science fiction and genre shows (as with *Babylon 5*, *The X-Files*, and *Buffy the Vampire Slayer*, to name three).

One of the first broadcast network shows of the serial storytelling revolution debuted in the fall of 1999, eight months after *The Sopranos* appeared to great critical acclaim. NBC's *The West Wing* took a gamble: creator Aaron Sorkin took the chance that America would tune into a narrative about presidential politics during one of the most politically polarized eras in American history. Sorkin's gamble paid off, and *The West Wing* enjoyed a critically acclaimed seven-year run and won dozens of Emmys.

More controversial—but also much more popular—was an entirely different kind of serial drama, one that proved that shocking violence need not be confined to the criminal underworld: Fox's spy thriller *24*, which began in fall 2001, played on public anxieties about terrorism in the wake of the September 11 al-Qaeda attacks and fed a debate about the use of torture in the real world. More than that, though, the show's mastery of high-tension action and clever structure (each season took place within the confines of a single day) won over millions.

The show that really signaled the transformation of television drama wouldn't appear until a few years later. When *Lost* first aired in September 2004, its success was by no means guaranteed; its elaborate special effects and location filming in Hawaii made it very expensive and very risky. But its fascinating characters, complex mythology, and accomplished blend of science fiction and soap opera made it a massive popular and critical success. *Lost*, which told the story of the survivors of a plane crash on a mysterious island, became the must-see show of the 2000s, and watercooler talk was galvanized by its constant twists and turns. It became such a phenomenon that newspapers and websites dedicated huge amounts of space to recapping each episode, analyzing every scene, and teasing out every hint about the enigmatic plot. This triggered a widespread transformation of the very nature of television criticism that continues to this day. Magazines, newspapers, and websites began supplying weekly recaps of popular shows, and TV reviews became a bigger draw than ever. When *Lost* ended, it did so with an episode that enraged a number of fans (a familiar sensation to viewers of *The Sopranos*), but it left its mark: it spawned dozens of imitators and changed the way people watched TV.

SONS OF ANARCHY: MOB WARFARE ON WHEELS

A little more than a year after the final episode of *The Sopranos* aired, FX—a network that was only then beginning to make a serious claim as the heir to HBO's position as the source of cable's best original television series—debuted a much-hyped show called *Sons of Anarchy*. It wasn't the first program to be called the "new *Sopranos*" by fans, critics, or even a show's creators, but it very quickly made the case that it was the most legitimate claimant to that title.

Created by Kurt Sutter, a multitalented New Jersey native who had previously worked on the network's breakout hit *The Shield*, *Sons of Anarchy* clearly displayed the lessons it had learned from *The Sopranos* by combining extreme violence with engaging family drama, but also brought its own combination of highbrow and lowbrow flavor to the recipe: it borrowed its plot structure from no less respectable a source than Shakespeare's *Hamlet*, but peppered its narrative with low-down sex, bloody criminal misdeeds, and raw energy. Audiences responded much as they had to *The Sopranos*, making *Sons of Anarchy* the biggest rating success in FX's history.

Much like the saga of Tony Soprano, *Sons of Anarchy* focused on a criminal subculture—the outlaw biker underground—that has seen its better days and is constantly threatened by the incursion of younger, hungrier, and more brutal gangs, as well as the unwelcome attention of federal agents. The Bureau of Alcohol, Tobacco, and Firearms stands in for the FBI here, but its methods are much the same: wiretaps, RICO suits, and the possibility that a comrades will flip and inform on the gang all make it difficult for the main characters to trust anyone. The leader is Clay Morrow (a majestic Ron Perlman); like Tony and Carmela, he and his wife, Gemma (a powerful Katey Sagal), see their actions through rose-colored glasses, excusing all their crimes and corruption by claiming they're trying to keep even worse elements out of their idyllic town. Gemma's son from a previous marriage, Jax (Charlie Hunnam), doesn't see it that way, though: his devotion to the Sons is tainted by his growing distaste for their activities and his suspicions that Clay and his mother may have conspired to murder his father.

Thematically, *Sons of Anarchy* covers all the bases previously tracked by *The Sopranos*: how loyalty can be divided between a real family and a surrogate family, the inability to develop real friendship and trust in an atmosphere built on lies, and the difficulty of getting out of a bad situation one was born into. But *Sons*, while no dramatic or technical masterpiece, takes off in rewarding directions of its own, which save it from being merely a cleverly executed copy. Its acting generally excellent (from the likes of Ryan Hurst and William Lucking, and a handful of *Deadwood* veterans like Dayton Callie and Titus Welliver). More important, Kurt Sutter is more willing to indulge fans' love of violence and chaos, spicing up the show with the kind of pulpy action that Chase tried to keep at arm's length. It usually yields rewarding—and distinctive—results.

BREAKING BAD BLURS THE LINES OF CRIME DRAMA

Those searching for a perfect example of the kind of high-quality television that could not exist without *The Sopranos* could not find a better one than AMC's incredible hour-long drama *Breaking Bad*. It not only took advantage of the post–David Chase world of serial storytelling and the technique of applying a wide-screen aesthetic to a small-screen program, but also picked up on Chase's new approach to the crime drama and took it to places it had never been before. Only a season after its 2008 debut, it was hailed as one of the best shows on television, and it has taken the idea of the criminal as antihero so far into new terrain that it has created its own unique vocabulary and rhythm.

Breaking Bad tells the story of luckless high school chemistry professor Walter White (played to perfection by an incredibly shaded Bryan Cranston), who is diagnosed in the first episode with untreatable—and terminal—lung cancer. Through a series of coincidences, Walter—who has done little to prepare for the future of his wife and his disabled son—discovers he can make a lot of money in a very short period of time by making and selling an especially potent strain of methamphetamine. Teaming up with an ex-student, he begins dealing meth and earning cash, only to discover that a life of crime is far more complicated than it first seems.

The virtues of *Breaking Bad* are literally apparent from its very first frame: the show begins with a heart-stopping action sequence that places viewers at a critical juncture in White's life with absolutely no background, leaving them in a thrilling free fall until all the pieces are finally put into place. And as the show went on, *Breaking Bad* proved to possess an absolute genius for this kind of thing—season after season, episode after episode began or ended with dazzling cliffhangers. But the quiet moments in between, in which Walter attempts to make sense of a life that is falling apart at every junction, where he relates to his wife (wonderfully played by *Deadwood* veteran Anna Gunn) and family, where his sickness as well as his method of dealing with it spiral out of control, are no less amazing, proving that the show's creators can deliver at any speed.

The man behind *Breaking Bad* is Vince Gilligan—he is a veteran of *The X-Files*, but clearly learned a number of vital lessons from *The Sopranos*. While Walter White is a man largely without greed, who enters the criminal underworld not out of selfishness or sociopathy, he, like Tony Soprano, must learn that he can't keep his home and "professional" life separate, that violent actions have violent consequences, and that the times you try the hardest to protect your family can be the times you put them at the greatest risk. *Breaking Bad* is a story of punishing highs and lows, but delivers a heavy sense of moral complexity behind the thrills.

Russell Crowe in *American Gangster.* (Universal Studios/Photofest)

9

WELCOME TO AMERICA: CRIME DRAMA FOR A NEW MILLENNIUM

GRAND THEFT AUTO IV

Throughout the Century of Crime, every artistic genre has expanded to accommodate the public fascination with crime and criminals. While this book has largely focused on movies and television, the crime drama can be found in almost every form of expression of the twentieth century: novels, short stories, plays, poems, songs, and operas all told the stories of legendary lawbreakers. Even crime-scene photographs came to be valued as much for their aesthetic qualities as their utility toward the end of the century, as the culture began to fetishize the past for its vanished style. So it is only natural that the emergent art form of the twenty-first century would manifest its greatness around the widely beloved format of the crime drama as well.

Of course, there are those who will still dispute that the video game is an art form at all. Respected film critic Roger Ebert touched off a huge Internet controversy in 2010 by expressing just that opinion. Metaphysical questions about the meaning of art are beyond the scope of this book, but it can be said that video games of the modern era certainly possess all the important qualities of an art form like film. Like a movie or a television show, a modern video game has a plot, a narrative arc, and a script with dialogue, written by an author; it has characters played by professional actors; it has direction and cinematography, and location, sets, and props that seem no less real for the fact that they don't exist in any physical space. And increasingly, video games fall into genres and have tones, moods, themes, and stories with beginnings and endings in which the characters' moral choices affect the ultimate outcome. With all these qualities in place, it seems churlish to quibble over the minor issues that separate games from other artistic media.

On a practical level too, video games are big business. Increasingly, they cost as much or more as the biggest motion picture blockbusters—and the most successful of them bring in as much money or more. Like big movie studio releases, they are developed years in advance and are released to coincide with key periods of consumer spending. Their characters are voiced by established Hollywood stars, and their stories are written by professional screenwriters. Their "cut scenes"—the computer-animated, nonplayable sequences that advance the narrative—can take up as much space in a game as the average television miniseries (2010's *Final Fantasy XIII* had over ten hours of cut scenes, 2011's celebrated *L.A. Noire* featured five hours and four more available via download, and 2006's *Xenosaga Episode III* had almost five hours just in its first half), and some of these are on their way to becoming as iconic and memorable as legendary moments in film. ☞

SUPPORTING EVIDENCE:
5 MORE MULTIMEDIA MOB CLASSICS

1. The *Underworld USA* Trilogy (1995–2009, USA; James Ellroy, author) The crime novel is a vast topic, stretching back well over a century and far beyond the scope of this book, and with a massive literature all its own. But those on the lookout for a modern literary manifestation of their gangster jones would be wise to start with this nihilistic, savage trilogy from the author of *L.A. Confidential*: 1995's *American Tabloid*, 2001's *The Cold Six Thousand*, and 2009's *Blood's a Rover*.

2. *The Crime Library* (1998–present, USA; Marilyn J. Bardsley, creator) Originally privately run and now hosted by the cable channel TruTV, the website crimelibrary.com is one of the most addictive on the Internet.

Contrary to the web's tendency toward brevity, the site's frequently updated material—complete with an huge section on mobsters and gangsters of every stripe—runs to exhaustively researched articles of near book length.

3. *A Prince Among Thieves* (1999, USA; Prince Paul, creator)
Hip-hop producer, DJ, and MC Prince Paul has always had a flair for the dramatic, so it's no surprise he created one of the most fascinating concept albums ever made. A hood movie in audio form, its story is as satisfying as its music, telling the tale of a young man desperate to make it big who gets involved with drugs and crime.

4. *Last Life in the Universe* (2003, THA; Pen-Ek Ratanaruang, dir.)
The surreal, languid, gorgeous story of a suicidal librarian whose brother is a gangster on the run from his yakuza boss, *Last Life in the Universe* is a wonderful introduction to the new world of international crime cinema. The mob action is kept to a minimum, but it's a fantastic film, and with its languages, cast, and crew drawn from Thailand, the U.S., the U.K., Hong Kong, and Japan, it's also indicative of the multinational flavor of an emerging pan-Asian tradition.

5. *Mafia II* (2007, USA; 2K Games, publisher)
Unlike some of its brothers, this organized-crime video game features nothing special in terms of game play. But its involving, complex, and authentic story of the rise of a young Italian-American mobster and its snappy dialogue are further indicators that video games may be the future of interactive entertainment.

The *Grand Theft Auto* series by the innovative Rockstar Games company began as a fairly simple top-down car chase game, but by the time of its third installment, the groundbreaking *Grand Theft Auto III* in 2001, the series had changed significantly—and dragged the gaming world into a new century. Introducing 3-D animation, a nonlinear narrative, an incredibly broad and deep fictional world to explore, and most important, the concept of "sandbox" play (allowing gamers to go places and do things whenever and however they liked, instead of following a restricted, one-way series of directions), *Grand Theft Auto III* revolutionized the entire industry.

Grand Theft Auto III was also immersed in the crime drama genre. With a heaping helping of satire and black comedy, it delivered the kind of thrills and action scenes one would expect from a well-done heist film, with its nameless, silent protagonist navigating a world in which riches and power were just one broken law away. Future installments wore their influences even more plainly on their sleeves. The 2002 follow-up, *Grand Theft Auto: Vice City*, was set in a lightly fictionalized Miami, and in addition to its top-rate celebrity voices (*GoodFellas* star Ray Liotta plays the main character, fallen mobster Tommy Vercetti), the game riffed on the crime-movie culture of the 1980s. *Miami Vice* was one of its touchstones, as was Brian De Palma's notorious *Scarface* remake. *Grand Theft Auto: San Andreas* followed in 2004, and proved to be the most ambitious installment yet. It featured a scenery-chewing Samuel L. Jackson as the game's main villain, an incredibly thorough re-creation of crime-ridden South Central Los Angeles, a pitch-perfect evocation of the gangsta-infused hood movies of the late '80s and early '90s, and the most sophisticated, nastily observant script to date from writers and creators Sam and Dan Houser.

It would be another four years before the next installment of the series would appear, but it would prove well worth the wait. Released just before Christmas 2008, *Grand Theft Auto IV* not only became one of the best-selling video games of all time, netting more than $500 million in sales in its first week, but also met with near-universal praise from critics both in and out of the video game industry. They praised not only its playability, graphics, and immersive qualities, but also less objective measures traditionally associated with . . . well, art. Its acting, story, and script all received great critical attention; it was cited not only in the gaming press but also in venues no less lofty than *The New York Times* for its mood, its tone, its unforgettable characters, and the remarkable complexity and verisimilitude of its setting (Liberty City, a doppelgänger of New York, complete with four of its boroughs). It was widely considered a masterpiece, and one that not only helped legitimize the video game as an artistic medium but also made a great leap forward from the parody and homage of previous installments, creating its own unique, original story.

Like *The Sopranos*, *Grand Theft Auto IV* was made up of the accreted influences of dozens of crime stories that preceded it. Each features elements that are familiar to anyone who has followed the history of the crime drama: a heist here, a caper here, a drug deal drawn from one movie, and a theatrical murder taken from another. But what makes both works special is their ability to synthesize familiar elements into something striking and dynamic. Both have a theatrical quality to their direction, but also benefit from long story arcs that culminate in dramatic set pieces—what *The Sopranos* accomplishes is the product of the hour-long television drama, while *Grand Theft Auto IV* pulls off the same effect by compressing months of storytelling into hours of game play and connected cut scenes. Both draw on the lessons of the past, but give them a modern interpretation driven by a very specific mood and a main character of great psychological depth.

The overall feel of *Grand Theft Auto IV*, despite its contemporary setting and shockingly precise duplication of modern-day New York, is that of the downbeat, depressed crime films of the 1970s, when the Big Apple was a cesspool of crime, poverty, and despair. It not only introduced elements of game play that gave the player the ability to make moral choices, but also ensured that those moral choices would make a difference—just as Tony Soprano had opportunities to do right and opportunities to do wrong, and each decision resulted in inescapable consequences for him and his family, *Grand Theft Auto* lets the player make similar decisions for the main character, which will end up having devastating repercussions as the narrative builds to its unforgettable and extremely downbeat conclusion.

The game's protagonist is Niko Bellic, a man who carries with him profound psychological wounds, much as does the head of a certain fictional New Jersey criminal enterprise. But Niko's wounds are deeper and darker than Tony Soprano could imagine. His early adulthood was spent in an unnamed Eastern European country, where he witnessed almost unspeakable atrocities during the wars that tore apart the Balkans in the 1990s. Left with deep scars, both physical and mental, he was unable to incorporate into mainstream society and turned to a life of crime just to survive. But there, too, Niko found no joy, encountering only betrayal, cruelty, and death. After a highly traumatic event, he finally decided to move to America at the behest of his brother Roman. Roman is a dreamer who lures him there with the promise of easy wealth, fast cars, fancy houses, and beautiful women, but when Niko arrives, he learns that this has been just another lie: Roman barely makes a living as the operator of a third-rate cab stand, and Niko is again faced with no choice but to reenter a life of crime. This time, however, he discovers a chance at redemption and a chance at revenge—but he must choose between them, because he can't have both.

Niko also finds cold comfort in the material rewards he wins from his life of crime. Much as David Chase used Tony Soprano's self-deluding behavior to illustrate the moral monstrosity of organized crime, writers Dan Houser and Rupert Humphries use the constant betrayals and rivalries among crime bosses to show us what a desperate and hollow life theirs is. Niko is no communist, but he sees how easily money, power, and consumer goods—hard fought over and paid for in blood—can be lost in seconds, thanks to one bad decision, turn of fortune, or run-in with the law. While he finds himself largely unable to rise to a leadership position within the various criminal gangs for whom he works, he doesn't seem to view that as much of a loss. He finds the bosses brutal, disloyal, distrustful, thoughtless, and easy to manipulate. Deeply distrustful and misanthropic, Niko sees what happens to the men at the top of the pile and finds himself wanting no part of it.

Niko Bellic is, in many ways, Tony Soprano's polar opposite. Tony is in love with his mobbed-up lifestyle, and while he sometimes feels constricted by it, he celebrates the material gains, the access to women and wealth, and the sense of power he gets from his position. Niko, on the other hand, is joyless and cynical, brutalized by his past and his own bad behavior; unlike Tony, who is constantly in denial, he can never let himself forget the terrible things he has done. He holds his fellow criminals in contempt, revulsed by their easy brutality, and despite his constant opposition to them, he respects the police as fellow professionals faced with a difficult job. Niko takes no solace in drugs, reacts badly to liquor, is turned off by loose women, and only relies on violence because he knows little else. Like Michael Corleone, he is constantly pulled back every time he tries to get out. But for him, the outside and the inside alike are dead ends filled with unhappiness, a walk down the same mean streets. He begins the game deeply cynical about the endless promise of America; he ends it even more so, having been drawn into the same hellish underworld he dwelt in overseas.

But despite the variance in their lead characters and the very different methods of their presentation, *Grand Theft Auto IV* and *The Sopranos* are decidedly of a piece. Both hinge their compelling stories on the psychological intricacies of their main characters, and both have a supporting cast of great depth. Both feature clever plots and give us a glimpse at a wide range of criminal activities and the culture of different ethnic mobs. Both go to great pains to make their settings extremely real to audiences—quite an accomplishment for the former, since it is not "real" at all—and present us with a world in which we want to spend a lot of time. Music is an integral part of each; the *Grand Theft Auto* games have always been extremely careful with their song selection, and their creators take pains to incorporate the tunes into the story to a degree that rivals *The Sopranos* and the films of Scorsese and Tarantino. Both *The Sopranos* and *Grand Theft Auto* signaled a major transformation in the way crime drama was presented in their respective media. If *Grand Theft Auto IV* can't convince fans of *The Sopranos* that video games are a medium with vast storytelling potential—a potential that is only now beginning to be tapped—then nothing will.

THE DEPARTED AND BOSTON CRIME

Boston has always stood in the shadow of New York—if you don't believe it, just ask a Red Sox fan. But that doesn't mean that Beantown doesn't have its own storied history of gangsterism and crime. Its great wealth, key physical location, ethnic tensions, economic disparities, and cross-pollination with the New York Mafia families placed it squarely in the same traditions of organized mayhem. American popular culture just took awhile to catch up. And it was, coincidentally, just around the same time that the Boston Red Sox finally began to shed their decades-long "curse" and see success in the World Series that America began to sit up and take notice of the rich world of Boston crime.

It had always been there, of course. Boston, like New York and New Jersey, is a wealthy, densely populated part of the coastal Northeast, and it is also home to a large number of ethnic groups with long, bloody histories in the world of organized crime. But though an occasional television show or movie took advantage of that history, Boston long took a backseat to New York in the public imagination when it came to organized crime stories. That began to change in the late 1990s and early 2000s, thanks largely to a number of crime novelists—foremost among them Dennis Lehane—who set their stories there. There had been stirrings of the Boston crime movie wave as early as 1998, with Ted Demme's *Monument Ave.*, as well as the Mark Wahlberg vehicle *Southie* and the 1999 over-the-top cult hit *Boondock Saints*. But the wave was truly touched off when veteran Hollywood presence Clint Eastwood adopted a Lehane novel, *Mystic River*, for film in 2003.

The genre reached its peak, though, in 2006, with the multiple Oscar winner *The Departed*. Director Martin Scorsese—whose name should be familiar to anyone who's read this far—stepped away from his normal surroundings and proved that his mastery of the crime drama extended far beyond the bounds of the Big Apple with his most critically acclaimed film in more than a decade. The story centers on Irish gangster Frank Costello (toothily played by Jack Nicholson and based on real-life Boston mobster Whitey Bulger), who places one of his best men inside the Boston police to keep them off his back, while the police place one of their own inside Costello's gang. It's a brilliant story, saturated in Boston lore, although curiously, *The Departed*'s origins couldn't have come from farther away. It is essentially a remake of 2002's *Infernal Affairs*, an exciting and highly acclaimed Hong Kong gangster film.

Many Boston crime dramas followed its release: Ben Affleck directed 2007's *Gone Baby Gone* (based on a novel by Lehane) and 2010's *The Town*; a sequel to *Boondock Saints* appeared in 2009; and Mel Gibson's *Edge of Darkness* (written by *The Departed*'s screenwriter) came out in 2010. *The Departed* remains the best of the lot, but the Boston crime movie is still a subgenre with some kick left in it.

AMERICAN GANGSTER AND REAL-WORLD CRIMINALS

With hop-hop culture becoming a global phenomenon and interest in crime films at an all-time high—and urban African-American filmgoers an emerging and desirable demographic—the time was ripe by the first decade of the twenty-first century for a new development. Blaxploitation was passé and borderline offensive, the hood film had played itself out, and shows like *The Sopranos* always stood at arm's length from black culture. One possible path was illuminated by the 2007 appearance of Ridley's Scott's epic *American Gangster*. It followed a recent trend toward crime dramas as biopics, treating notorious real-world criminals with the fascination and attention to detail previously paid to movie stars, political figures, and war heroes.

American Gangster tells the story of Frank Lucas—portrayed with a smoldering heaviness by Oscar winner Denzel Washington— who got his start as a petty criminal in Harlem, beginning as the chauffeur for numbers racket boss Bumpy Johnson and eventually becoming a crime lord in his own right. Lucas' discipline, business sense, and ruthlessness earned him great success, and he took advantage of his connections during the Vietnam War to smuggle heroin into the U.S. directly from Southeast Asia, forgoing the additional risk and cost of moving it through Europe in the manner of most New York mobsters at the time. The Mafia and the police alike were initially almost completely unaware of Lucas' activities, so tightly did he control his operation, but a few critical mistakes placed him at a dangerous spot, trapped between law enforcement and his fellow gangsters.

While Scott lacks the elegance and skill of a Scorsese or a Coppola, he hews closely to the set pattern of classic gangster epics and spices the movie up with the addition of sensational details drawn from real life. Lucas' story is one of overweening ambition, the deadly pitfalls of power, the untenable strain placed on families when they become involved with violent crime, and the way money can both motivate and ruin the people who sacrifice everything to pursue it. What is lacking in *American Gangster*'s plot and direction is compensated for in the excellent performances. Washington is predictably excellent in the lead, but Chiwetel Ejiofor as his brother and the venerable Ruby Dee as his mother shouldn't be ignored.

Frank Lucas had long been name-checked in the hip-hop world, and rap legend Jay-Z released a critically acclaimed concept album—also called *American Gangster*—at the same time the movie came out. But Lucas' story wouldn't be the only movie to win an audience and critical acclaim by weaving a sprawling narrative about a notorious real-life criminal: in 2008, Jean-François Richet released a two-part film about legendary French gangster Jacques Mesrine, and 2010 saw the debut of *Carlos*, a French TV miniseries directed by Olivier Assayas about the infamous Venezuelan terrorist Carlos the Jackal. As more and more information is unearthed and bigger and better biographies are written about high-profile criminals from every level of society, audiences are likely to see further films along the lines of *American Gangster*.

THE NEW WORLD OF INTERNATIONAL GANGSTER MOVIES

Just as crime has continued to evolve in the twenty-first century, so too have the ways, means, and even locales in which crime is depicted on screen. There will always be criminals, and there will always be people looking to tell their stories, but crime has an ever-changing face; everything from shifting demographic patterns to new law enforcement priorities to developments in technology has influenced the nature of the crime drama. Perhaps most important, though, the spread of market capitalism has not only created new types of organized crime, but also new generations of filmmakers in countries not previously known for their film industries and new audiences for locally grown crime dramas.

French filmmakers—once known for their elegant heist movies, existential films noir, and cool-eyed assassins—have started making crime films that reflect new social realities of international trade, urban violence, and desperate immigrants. 1995's *La Haine*, influenced by both *Taxi Driver* and American "hood movies" of the '90s, starkly portrayed the pressures of the impoverished, jobless youth of Paris' suburban housing projects. 2009's *A Prophet* is a mob prison epic in the old style with a new twist, with a young Arab working his way up through the ranks of the Corsican mafia. And again, Jean-François Richet's two-parter *Mesrine (Killer Instinct* and *Public Enemy)* is an outstanding look back at Jacques Mesrine, the notorious French gangster of the '70s, in the style of recent American crime biographies. Matteo Garrone's *Gomorrah*, meanwhile, tells an extremely different and decidedly unromantic story of mob violence in southern Italy, taking the Mafia epic in a distinctive new direction.

South Korea has emerged as a moviemaking powerhouse in recent years, and the best of its crime films blend traditional mob movie plots with the unsettling violence and eerie plot twists of horror films. Chan-wook Park's "Vengeance Trilogy"—*Sympathy for Mr. Vengeance*, *Oldboy*, and *Lady Vengeance*—are an excellent introduction, proving that Asian shock cinema can show American directors a thing or two about going to extremes in crime drama. Brazil, with its crime-ridden favelas and wide disparity between rich and poor, has produced a number of excellent crime stories in recent years, including *City of God*, *The Elite Squad*, and the documentary *Bus 174* (and a fictionalized adaptation, *Última Parada 174*). Romania has begun to produce some interesting crime films, including the irony-drenched and thought-provoking *Police, Adjective* by Corneliu Porumboiu. And though it's taken awhile for them to catch up in terms of mob movies—especially for a country founded by criminals—Australia has started cranking them out in quality and quantity: David Michôd's gangland epic *Animal Kingdom*, Nash and Joel Edgerton's clever neo-noir *The Square*, and the TV miniseries

Underbelly (the country's homegrown version of *The Sopranos*) are all outstanding. India has added gangster movies to the panoply of Bollywood styles. And the emergence of new cinema in countries like Austria, Thailand, and even Iran guarantees that the crime drama will continue to showcase new voices for many generations and generate new wellsprings of storytelling.

RED RIDING:
CRIME AND CORRUPTION IN NORTHERN ENGLAND

In times of moral panic, it is typical for crusaders to cite the negative portrayal of authority figures as a prime cause of corruption. The Hays Code was a perfect example: one of its directives was that law enforcement agents, from beat cops to FBI men, should not be portrayed as corrupt or crooked. This was, on its face, absurd; it was an open secret that the major reason organized crime thrived to the degree it did during Prohibition was the cooperation of bought-off cops. But when adhering to the Code meant the difference between a movie getting released or not, studios looked to the bottom line, and crooked cops became a rarity, appearing only in morally shady noir films from Poverty Row houses—and even then, they always got their comeuppance.

The pendulum began to swing the other way in the cynical postwar climate of the 1950s and thanks to the freedom of the youth movement in the 1960s. By the time maverick filmmakers came around in the 1970s, it was possible to make a movie like Sidney Lumet's *Serpico*, whose hero was abnormal for his honesty, not his corruption. *The Sopranos* was able to portray its authorities—police, politicians, and bureaucrats—at varying degrees of moral decay; even the well-intentioned FBI engaged in ethically questionable behavior to pursue their goals in the show. Street-level police corruption was taken as read in the post-*Sopranos* era, as reflected in movies like *Training Day* and television programs like *The Shield*. *The Wire* represented something of a zenith in its portrayal of even the best and brightest authorities being compromised, not just by weakness, vanity, and greed, but by systemic failures that called their entire purpose into question.

But no recent crime drama showed the collective weight of authority as so thoroughly rotten and utterly eaten away by villainy as the *Red Riding* trilogy, a series of TV movies made for the United Kingdom's Channel 4 in 2009. Based on a set of novels by the author David Peace (himself part of a rich new wave of modern crime writers from the U.K. that includes Jake Arnott, Ian Rankin, and Nicholas Blincoe), the films—*1974*, *1980*, and *1983*—span a generation. Tying in to real events that took place in northern England, and focusing particularly on the aftermath of the horrible "Yorkshire Ripper" murders committed by serial killer Peter Sutcliffe, *Red Riding* uses the basic facts to launch a dizzying, decades-long exploration of corruption in the highest places.

Red Riding is unmistakably dour and dreary; its moral tone mirrors the gray, wet, depressing weather of its setting, and northern England is portrayed, like Capone's Chicago and *The Sopranos*' New Jersey, as a place with its own rules that strangers run afoul of at their peril. No one—not the press, local businessmen, the police, politicians, or even the seemingly innocent—is shown as free of taint. But it is a compelling block of television that illustrates that the portrayal of corruption is a far richer dramatic vein than its denial.

BOARDWALK EMPIRE LOOKS BACK

By 2010, the legacy of *The Sopranos* was beyond question. It was routinely cited as not only a high point in the history of the crime drama, but one of the greatest television shows of all time. It had brought unforgettable new angles to the gangster epic, made stars out of its cast and crew, and overseen a profound transformation in the nature of narrative television. What could possibly come after? What could HBO possibly do as a follow-up, and where could the crime drama go from here?

The answer: it could go forward by looking back. Such was the thinking of Terence Winter, the creator of *Boardwalk Empire*, HBO's new attempt to recapture the magic of *The Sopranos* and add some original twists to the formula. Winter, the writer of some of the best episodes of *The Sopranos*, knew a good thing when he had it: he brought in a number of that show's veterans to help him put together *Boardwalk Empire*. Best of all, he got a living legend of crime film, Martin Scorsese, to serve as the executive producer and to direct the first episode.

Steve Buscemi plays Nucky Thompson, a political boss in Atlantic City, New Jersey, who consolidates his power through bribery, violence, and a willingness to play ball with a tide of criminals growing rich by exploiting the newly passed Prohibition laws. He's based on a real-life figure, and throughout the course of the first season, we meet many more—men who formed the first wave of big-time American gangsters: Al Capone, Lucky Luciano, Johnny Torrio, Arnold Rothstein, and Meyer Lansky. The show explores the uncomfortable relationship between the legitimate law of police and sheriffs and the street law of the gangsters and political bosses, and the psychology that drove many men to crime when they returned from the horrors of the First World War to a country they no longer recognized. There are constant glimpses into the shadowy deals and illegal enterprises that helped shape the modern world—and, of course, plenty of juicy sex and murder.

There is no question that *The Sopranos* was a high-water mark in the long and storied history of the gangster epic. But *Boardwalk Empire*, as much as it drew on the tools and talents of its spiritual predecessor, proved there was still life in the genre and that it could move ahead by reflecting on its own origins. By using cutting-edge modern storytelling techniques to look back on the era in which gangsters became an inextricable thread in the fabric of America, the show demonstrates that our cultural obsession with the theory and practice of crime—and the outsize personalities who were its most dreadful figures—would carry forward well into the future. The Century of Crime may be over, but *Boardwalk Empire* is evidence that the love affair with a well-made story about the bad guys at the heart of the American myth would carry on into the next.

Vincent Pastore, James Gandolfini, Tony Sirico, Michael Imperioli, and Jerry Adler in *The Sopranos.* (HBO/Photofest)

Conclusion

CENT'ANNI

The Sopranos ushered out the Century of Crime in grand style and got a new one under way in a fittingly controversial manner. Its final scene may still be causing arguments well into the next century, but that seems perfectly appropriate—would it have made sense for such a groundbreaking show, full of themes of secrecy, self-deception, and mystery, to have gone out with a conventional ending that tied up everything in a neat, unambiguous package? Whether Tony Soprano lived or died; whether, if he lived, he did so in comfort and safety or paranoid misery; whether, if he died, it was a matter justice, vengeance, or accident—these questions may frustrate us, but they also remind us how deeply involved we were in his life, and that what we were allowed to share of that life should be enough. Still, even if we ever stop asking what happened in those final seconds when the music stopped, we will never stop wondering what comes next.

If we apply the question in its narrowest sense and ask what comes next for *The Sopranos* as a piece of art and entertainment, the answer is likely "nothing." While some television shows of recent vintage have been given second life on the big screen—including HBO's *Sex and the City*—we probably won't see a *Sopranos* movie anytime soon. Such projects are difficult enough to put together when a show is left open-ended; rumors of a big-screen follow-up to *Deadwood* started circulating the moment the show was canceled but have never amounted to anything. Similar rumors have buzzed around *The Sopranos*, and while it is true that its ratings were far higher than *Deadwood*'s and that an audience for such a movie would certainly exist (as testified by the existence of this book), David Chase has made it abundantly clear that he said pretty much all he had to say about Tony and his family in "Made in America." A spin-off or a remake is possible, but even if the right creative team could be assembled and the right approach could be taken, such a project likely wouldn't surface for decades.

In a more general sense, though, many people have wondered what is next for Chase himself. The creators of most other critically acclaimed shows have leapt right back into the fray after completing a major project, some with good results (*Wire* creator David Simon's follow-up, *Treme*) and some with bad (*Deadwood* creator David Milch's follow-up, *John from Cincinnati*). But Chase has stayed far out of the spotlight; as of this writing, he hasn't written or produced anything since the end of *The Sopranos*. He has also given very few interviews and generally avoided any of the media attention showered on a creator of his stature. While the stars of his show have gone on to fame and fortune in other roles, and his writers, directors, and producers have moved on to their own passion projects, he has used the wealth and status afforded him by the show's success to keep himself out of the picture. Five years is an eternity to lie low in a field as competitive as the entertainment industry, which forever lusts for the next big thing, but if anyone can be said to have earned the break, surely it is David Chase.

Still, for all his earned success, Chase has been in the business almost forty years, and he didn't arrive at his current position because of a lack of ambition. Even age sixty-five, he surely has a few tricks left up his sleeve. The first post-*Sopranos* project he has been connected to is *A Ribbon of Dreams*, planned as a miniseries by HBO about two men who become partners in the early days of the motion picture industry and follow its development all the way to the present. This seems like a perfect project for Chase, and it would make an interesting companion piece to the network's *Boardwalk Empire*, but little information has come out about it, and its status is unclear. More certain is the future of *Twylight Zones*, Chase's first feature film. It's a Paramount production about a father and son in

1960s New Jersey, focusing on the sacrifices the father made so that his son, who becomes a rock singer, could succeed. A cast (featuring John Magaro, Lisa Lampanelli, Brad Garrett, Bella Heathcote, and none other than James Gandolfini in the lead role) has been announced, and Steven Van Zandt will produce and handle music for the film. *Twylight Zones* is tentatively scheduled for a summer 2012 release.

Leaving behind the specific and moving into the general, what does the future hold for the medium that *The Sopranos* so utterly transformed? What's next for the crime drama? It's a two-part question, really—what's next for crime and what's next for drama? Any attempts to guess will make future editions of this book look foolish, but it would be remiss to examine the works that led up to *The Sopranos* without considering what might follow in its wake. Predicting the future is always a gamble, but where would crime movies be without gambling?

Crime certainly *has* a future. While crime rates in America have been in a decade-long downturn, no society has ever fully rid itself of lawlessness, and unfortunately, some aspects of crime, especially in other countries, are worse than ever. As America's economy worsens, it is hard to predict the effect on crime rates; historically, crime always goes up during financial downturns, but the economic crisis that began in 2008 hasn't reflected this. (Of course, economic hard times don't mean a lack of interest in crime movies; the Great Depression is evidence of that.) Crime is still generally low in the U.S., but elsewhere, that isn't the case. Mexico in particular has seen its drug wars spiral beyond all reasonable control: in some parts of the country, drug cartels operate with near impunity. Murder, kidnapping, and bribery are the order of the day, and the cartels are so emboldened that they engage in open warfare against the government and the police, crossing a line criminals usually refuse to. Economic instability has also led to increases in the crime rate overseas, with many European countries seeing statistical spikes; and the new status quo of the European Union, with its open borders and its single currency, has led to a cultural cross-pollination of organized crime, with outfits formerly isolated in Greece, Eastern Europe, and the Balkans finding their way to Western Europe and the British Isles. Post-Soviet Russia, too, continues to be plagued by organized crime, and its crime bosses simultaneously consolidate their power into legitimate enterprises at home while sinking their claws into new areas of illegal activity in Europe, Asia, and America.

Whatever the future of organized crime, it may not involve the Mafia. While it has been the favorite subject of American crime dramas for the last forty years, for various reasons, both *La Cosa Nostra* in the United States and its Italian counterpart overseas are beginning to lose their grip. Crackdowns on mob activity both here and in Italy have nearly crippled the mob, and those Mafiosi who remain are mere shadows of their former selves, in terms of power and influence. When the FBI announced the largest Mafia bust in American history, it showed the general public what *The Sopranos* hinted at, what *Ghost Dog: The Way of the Samurai* played for laughs, and what *Gomorrah* played as grim reality. The 127 people charged in New York, New Jersey, and Italy bore little resemblance to the sinister, potent assassins and heavies of mob lore; they were largely a collection of second-rate thugs, some of whom were sick and many of whom were old. The average age of the higher-ranking members was well over seventy, and while the charges ranged from murder to drug trafficking, many had to do with petty crimes that seemed unworthy of the heirs to Vito Corleone.

In another sense, the Mafia is a victim of its own success. While the old bosses may cling to the old ways and the bottom-feeders may scramble to hold on to the scraps left at the table, many other mobsters have fulfilled Michael Corleone's dream and Tony Soprano's nightmare: they've gone straight. The most successful mob bosses have simply invested their money and applied their influence where it does the most good, in legitimate business (exhibit A: Las Vegas). While construction, transportation, and sanitation were once fronts for shady mob dealings, the smarter operators came to realize they could make more money running those businesses legally and avoid criminal prosecution to boot. The stock market might be a risk, but not as great a risk as dealing cocaine or hijacking trucks. Further, the events of September 11 affected the Mafia as much as they did every other aspect of American life. The FBI has largely switched its focus from dealing with organized crime to preventing domestic terrorism, and this has caused a major shift in the last decade of crime drama; terror plots have become a major element of police procedurals and have even inspired entire series, like *24* and *Sleeper Cell*. This new reality was a plot element in the final season of *The Sopranos*, with Tony's FBI handlers appearing willing to help him out in his war against the Lupertazzi family in exchange for information he fed them about a pair of Middle Eastern regulars at the Bada Bing; it also showed up in *The Wire*, when Detective McNulty—unable to get any assistance from the feds on a major drug case—observed: "All of them mopes in bracelets and not one named Osama."

Then again, it may be too soon to count out the Mafia. It has been operating in one form or another for over 150 years. It has survived wars, judicial crackdowns, federal prosecution, the end of Prohibition, the rise of the RICO Act and introduction of electronic surveillance, and the incursion of dozens of other ethnic gangs. Its members might just manage to survive getting old and going straight. If nothing else, they've proved remarkably adept at finding new ways to conduct their illegal business; it seems like for every revenue stream they lose, three more spring up in its place. The more clever and adaptable mobsters have already moved into modern, high-tech forms of illicit trade, including Internet fraud, electronic money laundering, online gambling, digital piracy, and all manner of Wall Street chicanery.

Such high-technology capers may point the way not only to the future of the Mafia, but also the future of Mafia-based entertainment. As discussed in the chapter about *Grand Theft Auto IV*, video games are beginning to compete with, if not surpass, movies and television as an entertainment delivery system. And crime-oriented games are among the most popular—aside from the *Grand Theft Auto* series, a highly successful video game version of *The Godfather* has been released, as has a game based on *The Sopranos*. *Mafia Wars* became one of the most popular social-networking games; and recently, crime games have become as specialized and niche-oriented as crime films, with the film noir–flavored *L.A. Noire*, the British heist–themed *The Getaway*, and the urban gangster epic *Saints Row* all selling extremely well. As video game budgets get bigger, casts more star-studded, plots more complex, and play more immersive, fans of the crime drama will be able to engage in the long sought-after but never realized ideal: they will be able to live as vicariously as possible the lives of big-time crime bosses, running their own criminal empires without any risk of jail time, their only victims composed of electronic pixels.

Technology will also streamline the process of watching mob movies. Streaming video and the integration of televised entertainment into the Internet are already making major changes in the way we consume culture. Twenty years ago, this book would have taken far longer to write; in the predigital era, tracking down obscure titles could take months. Now, it's possible to watch a movie—or even the entire run of a TV series—via a digital stream and then to get an instant recommendation for a work with the same director, actors, writers, themes, or in the same genre and watch it as well, without leaving the house or even walking to the mailbox. (All the films and television shows referred to in this book were available for purchase or rental either on DVD or via streaming media at the time it went to press.) The great gangster films of the past are now no longer legends spoken of only by aging movie critics; they are alive and lively and watchable in our living rooms. The game-changing new crime movies from Europe, Asia, and elsewhere don't have to wait decades to be seen; they arrive, streaming on your TV, within months of release. *The Sopranos* appeared in the early days of the Internet (witness Meadow showing A. J. a crude-looking website about the Mafia in the first season), but now you can pull up a list of all the great musical cues from each episode and download those songs within minutes to create a personalized *Sopranos* playlist.

The future of mob movies, though, may not entirely consist of forward-looking new technologies. The past is still a tremendously rich vein for storytellers, as evidenced by *Boardwalk Empire*, *American Gangster*, Michael Mann's *Public Enemies*, and other shows and movies. A side effect of the digital age has been to put a great deal of information about previously obscure persons on the Internet, where it is available to anyone. No doubt a whole new generation of young storytellers is even now discovering little-known events in the history of organized crime and thinking what a great movie those would make. Relatively recent developments in organized crime, such as the flourishing of black street gangs, the post-Soviet rise of the Russian mafia, and the dawn of cybercrime, are beginning to be thoroughly documented and researched, providing fodder for any number of future filmmakers. And on a more morbid note, many of the legendary figures of past eras of organized crime are starting to die off—too bad for them, but a lucky break for anyone seeking to tell their stories on screen but worried about lawsuits. (Studios too, forever looking to cut costs, have begun to look to the past, but not for stories previously untold—just the opposite. Sequels, remakes, reimaginings, and reboots are Hollywood's stock in trade these days, and the fact that the industry would much rather tell the same story again and again than take a chance on something new is both a problem and an opportunity.)

Our postmodern world has also equipped us with the tools and the tendency to create new art by cleverly combining elements of existing works. The mash-up culture has led to some fascinating developments in film and television—audacious storytellers blending one genre with another. Beloved TV writer Joss Whedon won over viewers with his short-lived cult hit *Firefly*, which cleverly folded Old West drama into a science-fiction setting. In 2005, a young director named Rian Johnson won critical praise for *Brick*, a hugely entertaining film that took the hard-boiled detective story, saturated with noir sensibilities, and fed it into a high-school romance. Christopher Nolan's unexpected 2010 smash hit *Inception* had all the elements of a classic heist film: the impossible mission, the hunted hero, the motley team of experts, the ticking clock—but it combined them with a science-fiction conceit (the team of experts are adept not at robbing banks or cracking safes, but at digging information out of a target's dreams) and a hefty dose of enigmatic philosophical and psychological speculation. Since crime is an omnipresent factor in society, this sort of combo-pack genre crossover will prove to be a plentiful source for future films.

One thing is for certain: the most fundamental change introduced by *The Sopranos*—the shift in emphasis for television storytelling from episodic to serial narrative—isn't going away. Episodic TV is still very popular, especially in the case of police procedurals, but increasingly, the shows that get the most critical attention are those that adapt the long-form story arcs and novelistic narratives pioneered by *The Sopranos*. We've already discussed a number of successful crime dramas that have arisen in its wake—*The Wire*, *Breaking Bad*, *Boardwalk Empire* and *Sons of Anarchy* in particular—but there are many more: *Justified*, *Dexter*, *True Blood*, *The Killing*, and the short-lived but highly acclaimed *Terriers* have all more or less followed this pattern. Allowing as it does for involving stories, long-term plot development, and deep characterization, the serial shift represents a major achievement in raising the quality and potential of television programming.

As this book has strived to show, *The Sopranos* is not responsible for everything admirable in the history of the crime drama. It is both an heir and a sire to many traditions. But it occupies an almost unique cultural nexus: it is a work of indisputably high quality that had the good fortune to appear at just the right time and place—and that, in conjunction with its own excellent attributes, made it seem like the culmination of a century's worth of worthwhile art in its genre. The combined products of the Century of Crime can be hard to trace, just like the loot from a perfect heist, and even here we've barely scratched the surface. But we've also provided a road map for *Sopranos* fans to follow in search of further payoffs and rewards; you will certainly find your own detours and side routes along the way that prove just as profitable. To David Chase, then, and to the people who made his astonishing vision come to life—and to you who have followed his path—we end with a traditional Italian toast that can be heard coming from the mouths of both Connie Corleone and Carmela Soprano: *Cent'anni*. May we live a hundred years. A century of crime has ended with the story of Tony Soprano; here's to another.

APPENDIX A:
TRACKING TONY: THE SOPRANOS FAMILY TIES

Having spent some time getting to know the various ele-ments that influenced the creation of *The Sopranos*, readers might wish to know more about the careers of the men and women who actually made the show happen. While *The Sopranos* marked the peak of many careers, its cast and crew were talented individuals who turned in outstanding work prior to its debut in 1999 and after its final episode wrapped in 2007. This appendix will recommend a few avenues worth pursuing in the résumés of the more prominent members of the Soprano family tree, as well as a few paths leading from the show's most memorable moments to destinations among some of the programs that make up its considerable cultural legacy. Use it to guide your post-*Sopranos* viewing, or just as a batch of items for your wish list.

Family Member: Lorraine Bracco
Position: Played Dr. Jennifer Melfi
Key Pre-*Sopranos* Work: *GoodFellas*. Playing Karen, the Jewish wife of Henry Hill in Martin Scorsese's 1990 gangland master-piece, netted her the role of Dr. Melfi and marked the first feminist portrayal of a mob wife in film history.
Key Post-*Sopranos* Work: *Rizzoli & Isles*. Bracco's first regular show after the end of *The Sopranos* was this TNT police procedural, based on a series of mystery novels by Tess Gerritsen. She plays the scrappy mother of the lead detective.

Family Member: Steve Buscemi
Position: Played Tony Blundetto; directed four episodes of *The Sopranos*
Key Pre-*Sopranos* Work: *Fargo*. Writer, director, actor, and former firefighter Buscemi has done some fine work with the Coen brothers, but his greatest was as high-strung, frustrated kidnapper Carl Showalter in this dark crime drama.
Key Post-*Sopranos* Work: *Queer*. Buscemi has done exceptional acting work (playing the lead in *Boardwalk Empire*) since *The Sopranos* and has done more directing—including an upcoming job helming this William S. Burroughs adaptation.

Family Member: David Chase
Position: Creator, head writer, and showrunner of *The Sopranos*
Key Pre-*Sopranos* Work: *Northern Exposure*. Though this quirky light comedy about a sophisticated New York doctor trapped in a small Alaska town couldn't be more different from *The Sopranos*, Chase was its executive producer for three years.
Key Post-*Sopranos* Work: Chase has lain low since *The Sopranos*. He's hard at work on a feature film entitled *Twylight Zones*, the story of a kid growing up in 1960s New Jersey who becomes a rock 'n' roll star.

Family Member: Dominic Chianese
Position: Played Corrado "Uncle Junior" Soprano
Key Pre-*Sopranos* Work: *The Godfather Part II*. Chianese has a long and storied career as an actor, but before *The Sopranos*, he was best known for playing Johnny Ola, the "Sicilian messenger boy" of Jewish mobster Hyman Roth, in this masterful film.
Key Post-*Sopranos* Work: *Ungrateful Heart*. Chianese, a Broadway veteran, is also a skillful singer and guitarist; on this 2003 album, he applies his talents to a set of traditional Neapolitan love songs.

Family Member: Allen Coulter
Position: Directed a dozen episodes of *The Sopranos*
Key Pre-*Sopranos* Work: *Sex and the City*. Though he'd directed

television for a decade, and honed his chops on *New York Undercover*, Coulter's first HBO work was tonally very different: helming eight episodes of the adventures of Carrie Bradshaw.
Key Post-*Sopranos* Work: *Remember Me.* Coulter had limited experience with big-screen features, but this 2010 romance was a runaway success, thanks to the popularity of its star, *Twilight* lead man Robert Pattinson.

Family Member: Edie Falco
Position: Played Carmela Soprano
Key Pre-*Sopranos* Work: *Oz.* An intense prison drama, *Oz* was one of the most highly praised HBO original series to appear before the debut of *The Sopranos*. Falco had a recurring and memorable role as corrections system officer Diane Wittlesey.
Key Post-*Sopranos* Work: *Nurse Jackie.* Falco followed strength with strength, going straight from *The Sopranos* to a critically acclaimed role as a New York emergency room nurse in this medical drama tinged with black humor.

Family Member: James Gandolfini
Position: Played Tony Soprano
Key Pre-*Sopranos* Work: *True Romance.* This stylish crime drama/romance was directed by Tony Scott and features an early screenplay by Quentin Tarantino; Gandolfini has a minor but memorable role as the cynical hit man Virgil.
Key Post-*Sopranos* Work: *Where the Wild Things Are.* The adaptation of a beloved children's bedtime story may be the last place you'd expect Tony Soprano to show up, but he's wonderful as the monstrous creature Carol.

Family Member: Michael Imperioli
Position: Played Christopher Moltisanti
Key Pre-*Sopranos* Work: *Summer of Sam.* Imperioli is a prolific actor and also a writer and director; his finest work outside *The Sopranos* was the script for Spike Lee's dark, underrated film about New York in the says of the Son of Sam killer.

Key Post-*Sopranos* Work: *Detroit 1-8-7*. Imperioli has been remarkably busy since the end of *The Sopranos*, and some of his best acting work came leading a very strong ensemble cast in this short-lived series about Detroit's police robbery-homicide division.

Family Member: Joe Pantoliano
Position: Played Ralph Cifaretto
Key Pre-*Sopranos* Work: *Bound*. The New Jersey actor known as "Joey Pants" has a diverse and proud career as an actor dating back to the mid-'70s, and one of his best roles is as the violent mobster Caesar in this cult crime thriller.
Key Post-*Sopranos* Work: *Percy Jackson & the Olympians: The Lightning Thief*. Pantoliano turned up as part of an ensemble cast as Gabe Ugliano in this highly successful movie version of the young-adult novel, directed by Chris Columbus.

Family Member: Steve Schirripa
Position: Played Bobby Baccalieri
Key Pre-*Sopranos* Work: *Fear and Loathing in Las Vegas*. Although it's a blink-and-you'll-miss-it bit part, much like his film debut in Martin Scorsese's *Casino*, Schirripa delivers one of his first performances in this excellent Terry Gilliam film.
Key Post-*Sopranos* Work: *The Secret Life of the American Teenager*. It may be an odd place for a former Mafioso to turn up, but Schirripa plays the father of Ben on the hit ABC Family Channel show about the travails of contemporary adolescents.

Family Member: Jamie-Lynn Sigler
Position: Played Meadow Soprano
Key Pre-*Sopranos* Work: *A Brooklyn State of Mind*. Sigler's first film role, at age seventeen, was in this little-seen but worthwhile indie film about the travails of a midlevel mobster—which also featured her future co-star Vincent "Big Pussy" Pastore.
Key Post-*Sopranos* Work: *Entourage*. A lad-mag favorite, Sigler has bounced around in several roles since *The Sopranos*, including

a stint on *Ugly Betty*. But her highest-profile role was on another HBO show, where she played . . . herself.

Family Member: Timothy Van Patten
Position: Director of twenty episodes of *The Sopranos* and writer of "Pine Barrens"
Key Pre-*Sopranos* Work: *The White Shadow*. Before becoming one of the most reliable directors on television, Van Patten—a member of a famous Hollywood acting family—played a high-school basketball player, when he was only eighteen.
Key Post-*Sopranos* Work: *The Pacific*. A follow-up to the critically acclaimed *Band of Brothers*, this harrowing miniseries about the conflict against Japan in World War II aired on HBO in 2010; Van Patten directed three of its best episodes.

Family Member: Steven Van Zandt
Position: Played Silvio Dante
Key Pre-*Sopranos* Work: The E Street Band. Best known as a musician, Van Zandt was a longtime member of Bruce Springsteen's band, playing and lending production assistance to albums like *Born to Run* and *Darkness on the Edge of Town*.
Key Post-*Sopranos* Work: *Little Steven's Underground Garage*. For the last eight years, Van Zandt has hosted a widely syndicated radio show featuring rock, soul, and blues and informed by his encyclopedic knowledge of music history.

Family Member: Matthew Weiner
Position: Writer of a dozen episodes of *The Sopranos*
Key Pre-*Sopranos* Work: *Andy Richter Controls the Universe*. Though better known for drama than comedy, one of Weiner's pre-*Sopranos* jobs was as a writer and producer for this short-lived cult-favorite sitcom featuring Conan O'Brien's sidekick.
Key Post-*Sopranos* Work: *Mad Men*. Taking many of the lessons he learned during his stint as a writer on *The Sopranos* to basic cable, Weiner created, writes, and produces this stylish, historically informed drama about a complicated adman.

Family Member: Terence Winter
Position: Writer of twenty-five episodes of *The Sopranos* and director of "Walk Like a Man"
Key Pre-*Sopranos* Work: *Xena: Warrior Princess.* Odd as it may seem, the writer of some of the finest episodes of *The Sopranos* came to the show directly from this campy, enjoyable syndicated action series about an Amazon barbarian.
Key Post-*Sopranos* Work: *Boardwalk Empire.* Winter created, writes, and produces this intriguing HBO drama, very much in the vein of *The Sopranos,* about political intrigue and criminal machinations in Prohibition-era Atlantic City.

Key Episode: "College" (season 1, episode 5, aired February 7, 1999)
Critical Detail: Tony comes clean to Meadow about how he makes a living—but not *entirely* clean, as he slips away from her college visits to exact revenge on an ex-mobster living under witness protection.
Next Step: *The Wire,* "Game Day" (season 1, episode 9, aired August 4, 2002). After months of pursuing crime boss Avon Barksdale, the Major Crimes detail, using varying approaches, interrupts a neighborhood ball game to get a glimpse of their target.

Key Episode: "D-Girl" (season 2, episode 7, aired February 27, 2000)
Critical Detail: Christopher's affair with a woman in the movie business gets him in the door to Hollywood, but after meeting with some movers and shakers, he discovers they have their own agenda.
Next Step: *Mad Men,* "The Gold Violin" (season 2, episode 7, aired September 7, 2008). Womanizing adman Don Draper has been carrying on an affair with the wife of a well-known comedian, but learns with a shock that her husband is on to them—and that he's the one being used.

Key Episode: "Pine Barrens" (season 3, episode 11, aired May 6, 2001)
Critical Detail: Paulie and Christopher find themselves in an increasingly perilous situation when a simple hit on a Russian debtor turns into a struggle for survival in the frozen woods.
Next Step: *Breaking Bad*, "Cat's in the Bag . . . " (season 1, episode 2, aired January 27, 2008). Walter White, a mild-mannered chemistry teacher turned meth dealer, must learn quickly how to deal with the violent side of his new occupation when a vicious killer is chained up in his basement.

Key Episode: "No Show" (season 4, episode 2, aired September 22, 2002)
Critical Detail: As tensions rise between the New York and New Jersey mobs, Paulie's imprisonment means a promotion for Christopher—which triggers resentment among the rest of the crew.
Next Step: *Sons of Anarchy*, "Patch Over" (season 1, episode 4, aired September 24, 2008). Faced with pressure from the Bureau of Alcohol, Tobacco, and Firearms and under attack from a rival gang, the Sons of Anarchy motorcycle club takes over a brother club—but not everyone is happy about it.

Key Episode: "All Due Respect" (season 5, episode 13, aired June 6, 2004)
Critical Detail: The conflict between the DiMeo crew and the Lupertazzi family threatens to spin out of control and erupt into full-scale warfare; Tony's only recourse to patch things up is to take out someone near and dear to him.
Next Step: *Deadwood*, "The Catbird Seat" (season 3, episode 11, aired August 20, 2006). As wealthy industrialist George Hearst tightens his grip on the western town of Deadwood and its considerable store of gold, he finds it useful to murder one of the most beloved citizens to prove he's serious.

Key Episode: "Made in America" (season 6, episode 21, aired June 10, 2007)

Critical Detail: The long and violent saga of Tony Soprano finally comes to an end—but Tony's ultimate fate is not clearly revealed, in what proves to be one of the most controversial television episodes of all time.

Next Step: *Lost*, "The End" (season 6, episode 18, aired May 23, 2010). The enigma of the final fate of the passengers of Oceanic Flight 815 is finally resolved, but in an unexpected way that also provoked greatly divided opinion among fans.

APPENDIX B:
ALL DUE RESPECT: 100 GREAT MOMENTS FROM A CENTURY OF CRIME

1. *Regeneration* (1915, Fox; Raoul Walsh, director)
2. *Underworld* (1927, Paramount; Josef von Sternberg, director)
3. *Little Caesar* (1931, Warner Bros.; Mervyn LeRoy, director)
4. *The Public Enemy* (1931, Warner Bros.; William Wellman, director)
5. *I Am a Fugitive from a Chain Gang* (1932, Warner Bros.; Mervyn LeRoy, director)
6. *Scarface* (1932, United Artists; Howard Hawks and Richard Rosson, directors)
7. *The Roaring Twenties* (1939, Warner Bros.; Raoul Walsh, director)
8. *This Gun for Hire* (1942, Paramount; Frank Tuttle, director)
9. *Double Indemnity* (1944, Paramount; Billy Wilder, director)
10. *The Postman Always Rings Twice* (1946, MGM; Tay Garnett, director)
11. *Brighton Rock* (1947, Charter Films; John Boulting, director)
12. *The Dark Past* (1948, Columbia; Rudolph Maté, director)
13. *Key Largo* (1948, Warner Bros.; John Huston, director)
14. *The Third Man* (1949, British Lion; Carol Reed, director)
15. *White Heat* (1949, Warner Bros.; Raoul Walsh, director)
16. *The Asphalt Jungle* (1950, MGM; John Huston, director)
17. *Gun Crazy* (1950, United Artists; Joseph H. Lewis, director)
18. *Night and the City* (1950, Twentieth Century Fox; Jules Dassin, director)

19. *Pickup on South Street* (1953, Twentieth Century Fox; Samuel
    Fuller, director)
20. *The Big Combo* (1955, Allied Artists; Joseph H. Lewis, director)
21. *Du Rififi Chez les Hommes* (1955, Pathé; Jules Dassin, director)
22. *The Phenix City Story* (1955, Allied Artists; Phil Karlson,
    director)
23. *Bob le Flambeur* (1956, Mondial; Jean-Pierre Melville, director)
24. *The Killing* (1956, United Artists; Stanley Kubrick, director)
25. *Big Deal on Madonna Street* (1958, Cristaldifilm; Mario
    Monicelli, director)
26. *Touch of Evil* (1958, Universal; Orson Welles, director)
27. *Pickpocket* (1959, Compagnie Cinématographique de France;
    Robert Bresson, director)
28. *The Untouchables* (1959–1963, ABC; Alan A. Armer, Desi
    Arnaz, Leonard Freeman, Quinn Martin, and
    Jerry Thorpe, producers)
29. *Ocean's Eleven* (1960, Warner Bros.; Lewis Milestone, director)
30. *Psycho* (1960, Paramount; Alfred Hitchcock, director)
31. *Blast of Silence* (1961, Universal; Allen Baron, director)
32. *Underworld U.S.A.* (1961, Columbia; Samuel Fuller, director)
33. *Youth of the Beast* (1963, Nikkatsu; Seijun Suzuki, director)
34. *Le Deuxième Souffle* (1966, S.N. Prodis; Jean-Pierre Melville,
    director)
35. *Bonnie and Clyde* (1967, Warner Bros.; Arthur Penn, director)
36. *Branded to Kill* (1967, Nikkatsu; Seijun Suzuki, director)
37. *Point Blank* (1967, MGM; John Boorman, director)
38. *Le Samouraï* (1967, S.N. Prodis; Jean-Pierre Melville, director)
39. *The Brotherhood* (1968, Paramount; Martin Ritt, director)
40. *Le Cercle Rouge* (1970, Les Films Corona; Jean-Pierre Melville,
    director)
41. *The French Connection* (1971, Twentieth Century Fox; William
    Friedkin, director)
42. *Get Carter* (1971, MGM; Mike Hodges, director)
43. *The Godfather* (1972, Paramount; Francis Ford Coppola,
    director)

44. *Black Caesar* (1973, American International Pictures; Larry Cohen, director)
45. *Mean Streets* (1973, Warner Bros.; Martin Scorsese, director)
46. *Chinatown* (1974, Paramount; Roman Polanski, director)
47. *The Godfather Part II* (1974, Paramount; Francis Ford Coppola, director)
48. *Dog Day Afternoon* (1975, Warner Bros.; Sidney Lumet, director)
49. *Dallas* (1978–1991, CBS; David Jacobs, creator)
50. *Atlantic City* (1980, Paramount; Louis Malle, director)
51. *The Long Good Friday* (1980, Black Lion; John Mackenzie, director)
52. *Scarface* (1983, Universal; Brian De Palma, director)
53. *Once Upon a Time in America* (1984, The Ladd Company; Sergio Leone, director)
54. *A Better Tomorrow* (1986, Cinema City Company; John Woo, director)
55. *The Untouchables* (1987, Paramount; Brian De Palma, director)
56. *The Killer* (1989, Golden Princess; John Woo, director)
57. *GoodFellas* (1990, Warner Bros.; Martin Scorsese, director)
58. *The Grifters* (1990, Miramax; Stephen Frears, director)
59. *The Krays* (1990, Rank; Peter Medak, director)
60. *Miller's Crossing* (1990, Twentieth Century Fox; Joel Coen, director)
61. *Twin Peaks* (1990–1991, ABC; Mark Frost and David Lynch, creators)
62. *Boyz n the Hood* (1991, Columbia; John Singleton, director)
63. *New Jack City* (1991, Warner Bros.; Mario Van Peebles, director)
64. *Hard Boiled* (1992, Golden Princess; John Woo, director)
65. *Reservoir Dogs* (1992, Miramax; Quentin Tarantino, director)
66. *Menace II Society* (1993, New Line Cinema; Allen and Albert Hughes, director)
67. *Sonatine* (1993, Shouchiku Daiichi Kougyo; Takeshi Kitano, director)

68. *Pulp Fiction* (1994, Miramax; Quentin Tarantino, director)
69. *American Gothic* (1995, CBS; Shaun Cassidy, creator)
70. *Get Shorty* (1995, MGM; Barry Sonnenfeld, director)
71. *La Haine* (1995, Canal+; Mathieu Kassovitz, director)
72. *The Usual Suspects* (1995, Gramercy Pictures; Bryan Singer, director)
73. *Fargo* (1996, Gramercy Pictures; Joel Coen, director)
74. *Profit* (1996, FOX; David Greenwalt and John McNamara, creators)
75. *Oz* (1997–2003, HBO; Tom Fontana, creator)
76. *Analyze This* (1999, Warner Bros.; Harold Ramis, director)
77. *Ghost Dog: The Way of the Samurai* (1999, Channel Four Films; Jim Jarmusch, director)
78. *The Limey* (1999, Artisan Entertainment; Steven Soderbergh, director)
79. *Summer of Sam* (1999, Touchstone; Spike Lee, director)
80. *The Sopranos* (1999–2007, HBO; David Chase, creator)
81. *City of God* (2002, Buena Vista International; Kátia Lund and Fernando Meirelles, directors)
82. *The Shield* (2002–2008, FX; Shawn Ryan, creator)
83. *The Wire* (2002–2008, HBO; David Simon, creator)
84. *Oldboy* (2003, Show East; Chan-Wook Park, director)
85. *Deadwood* (2004–2006, HBO; David Milch, creator)
86. *Brick* (2005, Focus Features; Rian Johnson, director)
87. *The Departed* (2006, Warner Bros.; Martin Scorsese, director)
88. *American Gangster* (2007, Universal; Ridley Scott, director)
89. *Mad Men* (2007–present, AMC; Matthew Weiner, creator)
90. *Gomorrah* (2008, 01 Distribuzione; Matteo Garrone, director)
91. *Grand Theft Auto IV* (2008, Rockstar Games; Dan Houser and Rupert Humphries, writers)
92. *Mesrine* (2008, Pathé; Jean-François Richet, director)
93. *Breaking Bad* (2008–present, AMC; Vince Gilligan, creator)
94. *Sons of Anarchy* (2008–present, FX; Kurt Sutter, creator)
95. *A Prophet* (2009, UGC Distribution; Jacques Audiard, director)
96. *Red Riding* (2009–2010, Channel 4; Tony Grisoni and David Peace, creators)

97. *Carlos* (2010, Canal+; Olivier Assayas and Dan Franck, creators)
98. *Boardwalk Empire* (2010–present, HBO; Terence Winter, creator)
99. *Justified* (2010–present, FX; Graham Yost, creator)
100. *L.A. Noire* (2011, Rockstar Games; Brendan McNamara, writer)

INDEX